MW00882404

The Quran and The Life of Excellence

The Quran and The Life of Excellence

Sultan Abdulhameed

Outskirts Press, Inc.
Denver, Colorado

Outskirts Press, Inc.
http://www.outskirtspress.com

ISBN: 978-1-4327-4021-4

Library of Congress Control Number: 2009940768

PRINTED IN THE UNITED STATES OF AMERICA

This book is dedicated to the memory of
Ehsanullah (1947–2007)
whose support and encouragement made
a crucial difference to me
during times of discouragement.

The Quran and the Life of Excellence

The Quran teaches how to live a life of excellence, to rise up to your God-given potential. We can either live by instinct, or we can choose to live by wisdom. The Quran speaks of God, angels, of life and death, but the purpose is always the same: to bring us out of stupor and push us into an awareness of the grandeur that is possible for all people. Prophet Muhammad is a role model for mankind because he lived his life at a very high level of excellence. He became a shining light for the world. You can also live your life at a much higher level and become a shining light to the world.

These essays were used to teach the Quran at weekly meetings of the Muslim Reform Movement in Brookville, New York, from 2006 to 2008. Each is a commentary on an *aya* or a set of *ayas*. (A sentence in the Quran is called an *aya*, or a sign). One of the essays was read at the start of the meeting, followed by a free discussion among the participants. The meetings are for an hour and a half so there is time for everyone to express his or her understanding of the wisdom in the ayas.

These essays are not in any particular order, and the most useful method to learn from them is to read them one at a time. It is more useful to read one essay several times than to read several essays together. This is because it is more useful to read and think about the wisdom in one aya again and again than to read several pages of the Quran with multiple concepts and insights.

Sequential reading, that is, reading page after page, and read in a quick manner, is a barrier to spiritual growth for most people. The ayas in the Quran were revealed over twenty-three years, one or two or just a few at a time. Each has a unique insight which can be accessed if we explore its message in depth, one at a time.

I wish to thank my wife, Safia, for her patience and support during the writing of this manuscript. The essays in this book are the result of a spiritual collaboration among those who have attended our weekly meetings and taken part in the discussions. Because each person has a unique life experience, a phrase of wisdom often pulls a different string in each of us. And when we share our individual perspectives with each other, a greater range of meanings becomes available to us. As we continue this practice week after week, everyone's perspective expands continuously. I have grown enormously by participating in these discussions.

English translations of the ayas given in this book have been influenced by those given by others, especially Muhammad Asad, Abdullah Yusuf Ali, Muhammad Ali and George Sale.

Our meetings are held in the community hall of the Brookville Reformed Church. I am grateful to Reverend

Allan Ramirez, the pastor of the Brookville Church, for the warmth of welcome we have experienced at the church.

If you wish to join our weekly discussion of the Quran in person, or by teleconference, please send us an e-mail via our Webpage www.mrmo.org.

Contents

1

Begin with the Name of God, the Merciful, the Compassionate

Bismillah-ir-Rahman ir-Raheem
(With the Name of God, the Merciful, the Compassionate)

The above sentence is prefixed to all the suras except one and is, thus, the frame through which the Quran sees reality. Everything emanates from the love and beneficence of God. Prophet Muhammad invoked the presence of God by speaking these words before he did anything, and he taught his followers to do the same.

The divine attributes *Rahman* and *Raheem*, mentioned in this phrase, are from the root: *rahm,* which is the Arabic for womb. Since your mother's womb is the place where you are totally taken care of, the word *rahm* is used also for the feeling of deep caring, compassion, mercy, and love. Now, in the rules of Arabic grammar, when you want to express an attribute with great intensity, you add the suffix –*an* to the root word. So *Rahm-an* is one whose love and caring are intense and unrestrained. And when you want to convey permanence, you add the suffix *–eem*. So *Raheem* is one whose love and caring is never-ending and unchanging. So we learn from this diversion into grammar that God is that Being whose love for His creatures is passionate and ceaseless. It is never absent and never diminishes in its intensity.

Recalling these attributes of God is to invoke the belief that the world around us is God's womb. All the nourishment we need for our sustenance and growth is provided for us in perfect proportions. We are protected and safe, and we are deeply loved under all circumstances. The challenges we face are like the push and pull that the baby experiences in the womb; they make us resilient and help us grow. There is development of the body in the first two decades of life, but the real purpose of being on the earth is spiritual growth. The experiences we go through are all devised to help each person see reality more and more clearly and to enable us to open doors to greater happiness and fulfillment for ourselves and others.

Now you can say, "Well, this is a nice idea, but it does not agree with reality. I have suffered in so many ways it will take too long to describe. I have suffered for no fault of my own. People have been unfair to me. Even those I have been good to have hurt me. These are the facts of my life. Where does the love and compassion of God come into this?"

There is no denying the fact of pain and suffering in your life. However, there is another important fact. Our beliefs are the forces that drive our lives forward. There is more than one way of understanding every experience. Some people see their glass as half full while for others it is half empty. Our deeply held beliefs establish how we see it. This choice then determines the decisions we make, how others react to us, and what happens next.

If we dwell on our past as if it were a tragedy, then that is what life becomes for us, and this belief conditions us to bring forth other such experiences. If, on the other hand, we choose to believe in God's beneficence, we will be prompted to look for and recognize the advantages that have come to us through what has happened. These two ways of thinking lead to very different paths in life.

It is a matter of great practical importance to adopt the belief that life is good. This, however, does not usually happen by reading an essay or in casual conversations. One has to focus persistently on the positive view of life. Many people can mouth words of optimism, but the idea stays outside of them; it is not what they feel inside. This can be changed by meditating on the divine attributes of *Rahman* and *Raheem*.

It works like this. Every day, spend some time alone in contemplation. And in this time, think about the ways in which God's caring has come to you. For example, I recall the time when I was a baby. I was helpless on my own, but God provided me with parents who took care of me. When I was sick, God sent people to help me and the sickness was healed. There was a time when I could not read or write, but God provided me with opportunities so I could learn. I remember the time when I had no income. I used to feel poor, but then things changed, and I became well-to-do.

Another aspect of this practice is to think of the specific events in your life today which make you feel good. I think of the person in my office who said good things about my work, the friend who called to say hello, the stranger who smiled at me, the paycheck I received, how my wife welcomed me when I got back home, the nice dinner we had together. There are an uncountable number of such instances, and recalling them strengthens my belief that my life is truly blessed.

I also recall manifestations of abundance that God has created around me. There is an unlimited amount of air to breathe and never-ending sunshine. The pleasure of a cool breeze on a warm day, the sight of buds opening in spring, leaves falling in autumn, a squirrel running in my backyard, gulls flying overhead are God's gifts of beauty and majesty.

As you deliberately engage the thoughts in which you have experienced God's gifts, the feeling of being loved becomes stronger and stronger.

If you do this contemplation on benevolence every day, you feel blessed. As you continue with this practice, you remember more and more events in which you were given love, care, and compassion. The feelings of gratitude take root in your heart. You begin to see that God has, indeed, been merciful and compassionate toward you.

As we meditate on the love of God for us, our spirits absorb more and more of it, and our dominant feelings are gradually transformed by it. The images of hurt and pain in our minds begin to fade. We feel happier inside. It becomes natural to smile. It is then easier to think well of others.

Having done this internal work, you can recall the feeling of God's love and mercy instantly, wherever you may be, by saying: *Bismillah-ir-Rahman ir-Raheem*. or, "With the Name of God, the Merciful, the Compassionate."

Whenever you say this, stacked up feelings of being loved by God are released inside you. You can recover His presence wherever you are and whatever the time of the day.

It is especially useful to recall God's abundant love when you begin an important task. This way, you approach everything you do with love. I see my role in everything I do as a conduit of God's love to the world. I love others, because I know that I am loved, and I want to share this gift with everyone.

This is a formula for a happy life. You can feel nurtured and supported by His love under all situations. By invoking God's loving presence, I always feel safe, and I know that no difficulties are too much for me.

2

Stages of Growth

Sura 84 Ayas 16–19
I swear by the glow of sunset,
And by the night as it gathers,
And by the moon growing to its fullness.
You will surely move from stage to stage.

The night appears quiet, but there is much change taking place. The glow of sunset gradually disappears, and the dark takes over. The creatures come back and gather in their nests. Then the moon comes out and grows in brightness. Nature unfolds in many ways during the night. In the same manner, people go through stages in their journey through life. While people often think about the visible changes from childhood to adulthood to old age, there are important changes also in the condition of the spirit as it goes from one level to another.

Three categories of spiritual awareness are identified in the Quran. The lowest is *nafs-ul-ammarah*, i.e., a person who is heedless or unmindful (12:53), unaware of the consequences of his or her actions. People in this condition are quite willing to lie and to cheat. They are self-serving and have little or no concern for others. People in this category are firmly convinced that their unhappiness is the fault of others.

This mind-set is clearly seen in little children but also in many adults. At the extreme of this category, most criminals exemplify heedlessness. But many respected members of society who are clever enough to mask their selfishness under proper speech and behavior are also in the state of *ammarah*. Some self-seeking people reach positions of authority and power through cunning and manipulation. There are people who say they love someone, but their love is manipulative and aims only to serve their own needs.

People in the state of *nafs-ul-ammarah,* or heedlessness, experience life as chaotic and sometimes find themselves in a jam. Because of unprincipled living, they can get into trouble with the law. Lack of discipline in habits causes them to indulge excessively, which can cause financial or health crises or serious problems in the family. Such unhappy events can make a person ponder and ask questions about the direction of his or her life. Often, family members may have been concerned about this person and have been trying to persuade him or her to change course. Such intervention can help transfer a person to the next category of awareness.

A person who seriously questions and analyzes what is taking place in his or her life is in the category of *nafs-ul-lawwamah*, that is, a self-critical or self-evaluating person (75:2). Questioning and analyzing what is taking place in your life yields answers on what you can do better. A self-evaluating person figures out that he or she could have avoided trouble by making different choices. Such a person becomes more humble and seeks advice. Soon, the self-questioning person learns to set goals for the future and determine what he or she can do to achieve them. A typical habit of such people is to make a list of what they want to do during a day and then evaluate how successful they were at the end of the day in achieving their goals. As they grow in awareness, the quality of items on their list improves and they become better at executing their plans. As this process continues, people become aware that life is deeper than they previously thought and the search for spiritual knowledge emerges. You realize that the keys to happiness are within you, and you become keen in search of them.

Contemplation is a method of learning about yourself. You sit quietly and note what thoughts and feelings run through your mind. Everyone has their individual patterns of thinking, but a few negative traits are widespread. For example, many adults have memories of hurts from childhood that linger with them. You were mistreated or abused by someone, perhaps a sibling, a parent, a teacher, or someone else. A painful experience from a long time ago plays its scene in your mind every day and makes you unhappy every day. This affects how you live your life and how you deal with others.

A sure way to overcome hurtful patterns inside you is to develop faith: faith that God is benevolent, merciful, and loving toward you. People with positive faith learn to interpret their experiences in an optimistic manner. They believe that events of pain, loss, or disappointment have benefits for them and others, even if how that can happen is not clear at the moment. They are convinced that there is no loss without an accompanying gain, and God does not close a door without opening another.

A person who has become convinced of the benevolence of God has attained the highest stage of awareness called *nafs-ul-mutmainnah*, i.e., the one who is blissful. A person in this category is unperturbed by events. For him or her, no problems exist, only opportunities to do good; there are no failures, only openings to learn at deeper levels. Prophet Muhammad said, *"All is always well for a person of faith. When something good happens, he is grateful, and when something bad happens, he is patient."*

How to get to the state of bliss is taught by the Prophet in this advice to his cousin Ibn Abbaas, *"Shall I teach you a phrase that is the key to heaven? It is to say: there is no circumstance and there is no power except from God, who is Mighty and Magnificent."*

It is to say to yourself that what has taken place is from the might and wisdom of God, and it has the seeds of great goodness, and then to busy yourself in finding and cultivating that goodness. The person who looks at all events through this lens is in bliss.

When someone makes the declaration of faith: *There is no god but God,* he or she acknowledges the principle that there is no power except from God. However, the declaration is merely the start of your journey of faith. You then have to do the work to understand your life according to this belief. As you make progress in this effort, you interpret more and more of your life as an unfolding of grace and benevolence, you become more and more blissful, you find peace. That is why people often say that Islam means peace. The declaration of faith contains the principle that is the key to personal peace and tranquility.

The categories of awareness are internal states and are not directly related to appearances. For example, many people who are particular about religious practice are in a low state of awareness. They can be dishonest and selfish and clearly in the state of *ammarah*. It is common to see people who go to the mosque, pray regularly, and fast during Ramadan, but their lives are chaotic. On the other hand, we also know people who are particular about religious observances and are caring, honest, and disciplined. Questioning and self-evaluation make the difference. Those who do prayer as a ritual without thinking about it do not progress. But those who evaluate to improve their actions move higher.

Some people start out as religious, but as they question themselves, they discard their religious beliefs. They say. "I am a good person so why do I have to believe in God and angels and all the claptrap of religion?" They have moved higher in awareness but are outwardly nonreligious. Many in this group, as they continue to think and evaluate pros and cons, eventually gain an understanding of religion and God at a deeper level. They now pray, not because it is an obligation but because they really want to.

There are many substages of growth among those who have come out of heedlessness. At an elementary level, a person becomes aware that one should not be abusive toward others because it is not good for you. A higher step is the realization that it is better for us if we are generous toward others. Then there is the knowledge that we actually need very little for ourselves and we should use most of our time and energy in helping others.

3

The Uphill Path

Sura 90 Ayas 8–16

Have We not given him two eyes, a tongue, and two lips?
And shown him the two paths?
But he does not attempt to take the uphill path.
And what will explain to you what the uphill path is?
It is to free the oppressed,
Or to feed in times of famine an orphan related to you or the helpless down in the dust.
Only then will you be among those who have faith, those who support each other on the path of patience and compassion.

Every day we have the choice of taking the easy way out of a situation or doing what our conscience points to, which is usually a more difficult path. In what we plan to do today, whether at work, or in the family or in a social setting, we can think of doing just enough to get by, or we can stretch ourselves to do the best possible. We can either have minimal expectations of ourselves or we can demand more from ourselves than others expect.

Have We not given him two eyes, a tongue, and two lips?
And shown him the two paths?
But he does not attempt to take the uphill path.

Our God-given faculties, the ability to see, hear, and speak, are enough to help us recognize the choice between taking the low road and the high road. The low road is giving in to laziness and being centered on serving our own needs. The high road is doing the best possible and aiming to make a difference for others.

Those who understand the wisdom of the uphill path always choose to do more than expected. These are the people who continuously grow in their capabilities. People who do physical exercise know that muscles grow in strength if you push them every day to do more than what is comfortable. As the muscles are stretched beyond their apparent capacity, it may not feel comfortable, but that is how you grow. The same is true of our psychological and spiritual muscles. They have to be applied strenuously in order to grow.

This sura asks us to live the paradigm of the uphill road by doing our best in uplifting the disadvantaged.

And what will explain to you what the uphill path is?
It is to free the oppressed,
Or to feed in times of famine an orphan related to you or the helpless down in the dust.

The word *raqaba* translated here as "oppressed"

literally means "the enslaved." Although slavery has fortunately been eliminated from the world, oppression, subjugation, and deprivation are rampant and beckon us to take action. The modern media have held up a mirror in which everyone can see the human condition. The majority of people in the world are poor, malnourished, lack basic sanitation and the resources to educate themselves and their children. With greater information, we have greater awareness of political oppression, injustice, and prejudice around the world. In many instances, exploitation and unfairness are ingrained in cultural patterns, many, of which, are sanctioned by interpretations of religion. We in the present generation have an unprecedented opportunity to support the forces of progress against injustice and poverty.

We also see a representation of this global picture in the microcosm of our own lives, in the family, at work, and in our social circle. We encounter people whose lives are limited by a lack of awareness, poor habits inherited from family and culture, apathy, and prejudices they are subjected to, or their own prejudices toward others. Every day, through our words and action, we have the opportunity to uplift people into a better life. We demonstrate our faith when we take on the difficult task of helping someone.

Or to feed in times of famine an orphan related to you or the helpless down in the dust.

Please note that the aya speaks of feeding people in times of famine, that is, when there is a great shortage of food. It is good to help others when you are well-stocked and secure, but the uphill road is in sharing when you yourself have little, that is how you grow in faith.

Only then will you be among those who have faith, those who support each other on the path of patience and compassion.

Faith is defined in this aya by our commitment to help others. In Sura 51 Aya 56, God says, "*I have not created the jinns and the human beings except that they should serve Me.*" God has created us for service. We serve God by serving His creatures. Whenever we help others in any way, we are demonstrating our faith in God.

Worship that does not lead to active interest in uplifting others is spiritual stagnation. It is not unusual to encounter people who have little interest in helping others but have devoted many years to ritual prayers and as a result, have become more and more introverted. It is reported in the book of Tirmidhi that Prophet Muhammad said that "*a person who is oblivious of prayer but is generous is nearer to God than a devout person who is miserly.*"

In everyone, there is the strong urge to be happy, to be established in life in ways that please us, to have dependable relationships and the financial means to be secure. And these are positive desires because they help us develop our life skills and the means to raise the next generation. But sooner or later, the search for deeper meaning emerges. We ask ourselves, "What is the purpose of my life beyond making money and raising children?" The only answer to this question which creates lasting significance is our commitment to be of use to others. We can orient our intentions to be a source of uplift in every situation—in the family, in the practice of our profession, and, indeed, in every encounter with others. The pleasure of God is achieved through such a commitment because He has placed us on the earth as His representatives so He can work through us.

4

Path to Bliss

Every human being is working to achieve his or her own set of goals with the hope of finding happiness. Sura 92 points to three traits of people who find bliss and their opposites that lead to a life of misery.

Sura 92 Ayas 4–10
Verily you strive for diverse goals,
And the one who gives,
And lives consciously,
And testifies to what is the best,
We will indeed make smooth for him the path to bliss.
But the one who acts miserly,
And thinks of himself as separate,
And gives the lie to what is the best,
We will indeed make smooth for him the path to misery.

The world is an experience of contrasts. We are all different in our personalities, and each of us experiences his or her own set of circumstances. Every human being has a list of what will make him or her happy. And they are striving to find what will make them happy. However, lasting happiness is achieved through the cultivation of a few universal attributes that transcend our short-term goals.

There is a distinction between short-term pleasure and a persistent state of happiness that is called bliss. We can obtain pleasure easily by taking a walk on the beach, having a nice meal, or going on a vacation, and it is good because it gives relief from stress. Bliss is when your consciousness is permanently anchored on well-being, in knowing that all is well and your happiness is not threatened by what happens outside of yourself.

Let us consider these attributes:

The one who gives

In every meeting of people, there is a giving and a taking. There are those who are predisposed to think of contributing to others, and there are others who think "What is in it for me?" This takes place in the home, at work, and in public affairs. Experience shows that those who train their thinking to be givers obtain their long-term purposes much more than those who are focused on taking advantage of a situation or others. If you go to work with the idea of being useful to your employer, of always doing more than you are asked to do, you will soon be recognized as a valuable employee. You will stand out in contrast to those of your fellow workers who think of their work as primarily a source of income for themselves. The way to build a lasting and happy marriage is to think of your spouse as someone you have decided to nurture under all circumstances. You are in this relationship to enhance and support the other person. Even if, at the beginning of the relationship, your spouse happens to be a self-centered person, your continuous and selfless caring will eventually turn the other person around, and your giving will create peace and tranquility for you.

Sometimes the word "giver" has been interpreted in terms of only money, but this is an unwarranted narrowing of meaning. Willingness to help others with money is a great quality, but it is obvious that giving is a more general attitude. We can give money, and we can also give time, attention, caring, affection, and encouragement.

And lives consciously

The word *taqa* has sometimes been translated as "being fearful of God," or as "doing one's duty." Each of these interpretations conveys the essential meaning but is unnecessarily limited. The attribute described here is that of becoming aware that there is an unseen reality within us and around us that is much bigger than our physical selves. A wise person is conscious that life is governed by spiritual laws and not by our whims or willpower. Everything we do or say has consequence. We need to grow out of beliefs that are limiting us and seek to learn deeper truths in order to find meaning and fulfillment.

One basic truth is that we are all connected. People are all different in their appearances and their experiences, but their basic urges are the same. The divine spirit is in everyone. If you have advantage over others because of your good looks or your race or ethnicity or because you have achieved success, it is a mistake to look down on others, to think of yourself as separate. Arrogance isolates us, and it brings unhappiness.

And testifies to what is the best

The world is a marketplace of ideas. There are many opinions and belief systems. A wise person chooses and supports what he or she finds to be the best for the greater good. It limits us when we support an idea just to validate personal, national, or ethnic pride.

One of the greatest hindrances to the progress of humanity is the tendency of looking at your religion as a matter of national pride, to insist that we are right because it is us, and others are wrong because it is them.

In order to grow spiritually, we need to free ourselves from identifying with beliefs simply because "it is our tradition" instead of seeking the highest wisdom. We must learn to shed prejudice from our thinking and always look for the greater good. Prophet Muhammad said, "*Wisdom is the preference of the person of faith; he takes it from wherever he finds it.*"

Note that the attributes described here are attitudes within our minds. We may go through painful conditions in our journey through life, but our inner state does not depend on others. It is determined by how we have trained ourselves to think.

Giving, being conscious, and testifying to what is the best are among the attributes of God. Thus, cultivating these qualities is the same as discovering the divine within yourself. Each of us has some awareness of the possibility of living on a higher plane. The purpose of these ayas is to invite us to this possibility. Each day we can evaluate how far up the ladder we have climbed. Each day we can strive for a level higher than the previous day. This daily remembrance takes us closer to the place within ourselves where divine attributes are internalized, our perspective is transformed, and joy and happiness flow in us naturally.

5

What Comes Later Will Be Better

Sura 93

By the brightness of the morning, and by the night when it grows dark,

Your Lord has neither forsaken you, nor does He despise you.

Surely what comes later will be better for you than what came before,

And your Lord will soon give you that with which you will be pleased.

Did He not find you an orphan and has He not taken care of you?

Did He not find you wandering in error and has He not guided you?

Did He not find you needy and has He not enriched you?

Therefore, do not oppress the orphan,

And do not repulse the one who asks for help.

And recount the favors of your Lord.

Each of us goes through periods of pessimism, loneliness, or gloom when we feel that life is not working for us. Our efforts seem to go nowhere, and there is no help in sight. It is natural to feel pessimistic and hopeless in such a condition. Images of self-pity can come over us. Such thoughts deepen the gloom and paralyze our faculties.

We can overcome the depressing feelings in such times by recalling the successes of the past, the hurdles we have overcome. Each of us can think back to situations where the doors that were closed opened to new and better opportunities, by the grace of God.

The practice of recalling past successes lifts gloom and takes our attention to a brighter future. This is an important message in this sura.

By the brightness of the morning, and by the night when it grows dark,
Your Lord has neither forsaken you, nor does He despise you.

Just as nature never works in a straight line, our quest for happiness is not obtained by a straight march to our desired goals. Just as the darkness of the night alternates with the brightness of the day in the physical world, progress in any aspect of life is also like a wave, with peaks and valleys. In any undertaking, there will be periods of movement intermixed with stretches when we appear to be stalled in spite of continued effort.

When people go through tough periods, they often wonder how it can be, if God really loves them and takes care of them, as they have been told. Faith tells us that our Creator is always with us, with His compassion and mercy, during the night and during the day, during our episodes of happiness and unhappiness. His nurture works in ways which are beyond human calculation. His ever-present love assures us that:

Surely what comes later will be better for you than what came before,
And your Lord will soon give you that with which you will be pleased.

In a state of unhappiness, it is easy to think that there is nothing good to look forward to. In many situations, whether in your family, in business, or in public affairs, you will find people (sometimes these are experts) who make disaster scenarios for the future. But God promises to a person of faith that *surely what comes later will be better for you than what came before, and your Lord will soon give you that with which you will be pleased.*

God then reminds the Prophet of the several ways blessings have come to him in the past.

Did He not find you an orphan and has He not taken care of you?
Did He not find you wandering in error and has He not guided you?
Did He not find you needy and has He not enriched you?

So finds everyone else who has reached an age of maturity. Many of our needs have been fulfilled over time; many weaknesses have disappeared and are replaced by strengths.

It is very empowering to clearly validate this notion for your own self. A practical way of doing this is to think back about your life and divide it into five-year segments. Think about what your life was like in the first five years, between five to ten years, between ten to fifteen years, and so on, up to the present. In your journal, write a paragraph about what your strengths and weaknesses were in each of these periods. As you complete this exercise, you will discover the numerous ways in which unexpected help has come to you, problems have been resolved, and the many ways in which you have been pushed higher. You will know that you are, indeed, a blessed person.

The divine forces that have helped you in the past are still here and working to help you, and it is inevitable that your future life is going to better than the past.

The next two ayas then remind us that as we have been blessed, so we must bless others. God has created us to live and act as His substitutes on the earth. We live up to this mission by helping others, as God has helped us:

Therefore, do not oppress the orphan,
And do not repulse the one who asks for help.

The orphan in the ancient Arab society was the archetype of a helpless person. Watch out against the common tendency to be harsh toward those who are powerless. People who are in need represent opportunities for us to display the divine spirit in us. Therefore, do not give up the opportunity to help anyone. When we assist someone, we display the most magnificent parts of ourselves because we act out the divine attributes of The Giver, The Helper, and The Nurturer.

And recount the favors of your Lord.

In your thoughts and in your conversations, make it

a practice to recount again and again the many ways in which your life has been blessed, how you were weak and have become stronger, how you were sick and you were given health, how you were poor and became well-to-do, how you were plain looking and then became good looking, how you were ignorant and then became learned, how you were lonely and were given company, how you were confused but then found guidance, and the many other ways in which you were initially lacking but now have ease and abundance.

Note that this is opposite to the practice of a person who lacks faith. His or her conversation is remembrance of how misfortune surrounds them, how help has not come to them, how life has been unfair to them. Their worldview filters out the good that has happened to them.

God here recommends that we use a different filter. Remember the good part from your experience. This is one of the best ways to remember God who says: *"whatever My servant assumes of Me, that is how I am to him, and I am with him as he remembers Me."* Through recounting the help you have received, you will be internally and deeply convinced that you are indeed a blessed person. The feeling of gratitude will be a natural state for you. And in such a state, abundance of every kind will keep on showering you throughout your life.

This is the practice of Prophet Muhammad. There are thousands of his statements in the books of Hadith. A common theme in these narratives is that the Prophet always recounts the ways in which he has been favored and blessed. Mind you, he chooses not to be "realistic." He deliberately omits any mention of the pains and the losses he has gone through. He chose persistently to recount the favors of His Lord and in this way became an ocean of abundance for himself and for others. The same method is described here and is available to each of us to transform our lives.

6

Problems Are Opportunities

Difficulties, problems, and hardships are the stuff of life. Every living person finds difficulties in many areas of his or her life. Sura 94 explains their positive purpose.

Have We not lifted your heart,
And relieved you of the burden
Which weighed down your back,
And raised you in status?
And, behold, with every hardship comes ease.
Indeed, with every hardship comes ease.
Hence, when you are freed [from distress], resume work
And turn to your Sustainer with love.

To see the infinite reach of these ayas in human life, let us consider how ubiquitous problems and difficulties are.

The nature of man is to have desires. We are some place in life, but we want to be at a better place. This is the life force working in us. It pushes us continuously to seek a happier life. But whatever desire or goal you pursue, you encounter obstacles. For example, if you want to be healthier and look better, you have to exercise and change your eating habits, and that is difficult. You want to be highly educated and find it is difficult to get into a good school, and the really important classes are very hard. You want to start a business, but it is a lot of work to be organized and get capital. You want to get married, you meet many people, but do not find the type you want. You are already married, you find that your spouse is different from what you expected, and there are many obstacles to harmony. You want to be a leader in your social circle, and you find that everyone else wants the same also. You want to have a happy relationship with your parents, but you find they have unreasonable expectations. You want to be spiritual and start reading the Quran, but you find it confusing. These are some examples of the types of difficulties we face in everyday life whenever we want to move forward.

There are other more serious hardships that hit people unexpectedly and become like a *"burden that weighs down your back."* You are living your life normally and something tragic happens. There is a financial or political crisis or an earthquake or flood and you lose your business or home. You have a serious accident and lose a limb. You always dreamed of raising children, and you find that you can't have any. Your child is born mentally or physically handicapped. You discover that your spouse is having an affair. You become seriously and chronically ill. Someone close to you dies at a young age. In such events, it seems that God has decided to break your heart. People in such circumstances often ask, how can this happen if there is a God?

This sura teaches four principles of wisdom. Our outlook on life and its problems becomes totally different once we understand these principles. Let us consider them one by one:

And, behold, with every hardship comes ease,
Indeed, with every hardship comes ease.

Note that the aya is repeated for extra emphasis because it is so counter-intuitive. When people are engulfed in difficulties, they think there is no solution to what they are facing. You will notice that people who are not aware of this teaching spend a lot of time talking and obsessing about their problems to themselves and to others, again and again. They internalize the idea that they are stuck where they are because of fate, and there is nothing they can do about it. Many become emotionally trapped into thinking that their suffering is unique, which gives them special martyr-like status deserving sympathy and attention from everyone.

These ayas point out that every difficulty is accompanied by its solution. The solution or relief does not come *after* the difficulty, but is provided *with it*. We are often not able to see it when we are in the midst of a crisis, but it is there, which means that we can find it if we look for it.

This insight has important practical application. Once I recognize a problem that bothers me, I will benefit if I shift my focus away from talking about the problem to looking for its solution. I can say to myself, "What can be a positive outcome of this difficulty? What can I do to make this situation better?" Or "Who can help me in this?" Experience teaches that many times we don't find answers to such questions right away, but if we persist with an optimistic focus, answers are always shown to us. Getting away from repetitive recounting of our ills, by itself, creates relief.

The second important teaching in this sura is that through our difficulties we are raised higher. We become more, our strength increases.

Have We not lifted your heart,
And relieved you of the burden,
Which weighed down your back,
And raised you in status?

Look back at your life and you will notice that every progress you made was by overcoming a difficulty. You can be promoted to the seventh grade only after overcoming the difficulties posed by the sixth grade; you can go to college only after you resolve the challenges thrown at you by high school. You can get elevated to a higher position at work after you master the responsibilities needed for your present position. The progress of mankind as a whole is by the same principle. People found it hard to eat raw meat so they discovered fire and cooking. To overcome the fatigue of walking long distances, they learned to make wheels. The evolution of life also works by the same principle. Each individual in each species is stymied by some problems. Breakthroughs occur when someone figures out a solution. Problems, difficulties, and hardships are invitations to improvement and expansion.

The hardships we face are doors that appear closed, but they can be opened and lead to a happier life. God is like a coach in the gym who wants me to jump over the bar. He sets it high enough so that I will hit the bar and fall, until I figure out how to jump higher. Adversity and triumph are linked; they are two sides of the same coin. What matters is how we feel about the problems we have. If you can internalize the teaching in this sura, you will be able to create hope and positive expectation in your heart, even in the most distressing circumstance. As you gradually replace fear with trust, your life will expand and you will one day look back and see that there was an important purpose behind the pain you went through.

Hence, when you are freed [from distress], resume work,

When we are relieved of one difficulty, there is an improvement in our condition; we are stronger, but a new set of problems arise. This is because the purpose of life is to continuously expand the human spirit.

Understanding what this aya says is the main difference between someone who lives out his or her dreams and someone who does not. Successful people keep in mind that the adversities are there, so they then can grow and learn as they overcome them. Those who make a big difference in the world think of their problems as opportunities and go after them. Those who fail in life think of their problems as punishments and shrink away from them.

In the modern metaphor, this aya teaches us never to remain in our comfort zone. When one problem is over, get busy on the next one.

And turn to your Sustainer with love.

The most powerful resource you and I can have is to know that God cares for us and sustains us. The Arabic word translated here as Sustainer is *Rabb*. It stands for the one who cares, nurtures, fosters, looks after, guides, protects, shields, and cherishes. The guaranteed way to live a life of increasing strength is to remain conscious of your *Rabb*, the one who is not visible but always present. The hardships we encounter are shaped by our Creator as roadways to a better life. He has designed life such that problems always come with solutions. And He is with us and guides us through our difficulties.

7

Learn by Writing

Sura 96 Ayas 4–5
He has taught with the pen,
Has taught people what they knew not.

These brief ayas describe a powerful and practical, useful truth. The pen, or writing, is a source of knowledge. Through it we can not only express what we know but also learn what we did not know before—about ourselves and about the world. This is because through writing we can access the creative force that lives within each of us. Practice of writing expands our intuition and imagination, and it creates new perspectives.

All writers know this truth.

There is a widespread false belief that writing is for a special class of "gifted" people. This belief is there because in our present culture, only a few people write and they are called "writers." But the fact is that anyone who has learned to write can choose to write regularly. And the benefits of writing are so spectacular, and writing is so easy, that anyone who can write should write.

We are used to experiencing words when we speak and hear. We know that most of our power is through speaking and hearing words. With words, we can express our intentions and feelings and communicate with others. We communicate with God through words. Writing also uses words. But the value of writing is that it works through a different neural network in the brain than is used in speaking or hearing. Thus, writing is an additional avenue for expressing ourselves. It opens new channels to the soul and makes it possible for new insights to come to the surface.

There are many forms of writing, and each has value. But a type which does not require training and is of great spiritual value is "free" writing. Keep a notebook or a word processor file that you do not share with anyone. In it, write freely and spontaneously for a few minutes every day. Write what you are thinking. There are no constraints on what you write. Do not stop to correct mistakes but keep on going. Do not worry about grammar or spelling. Let it be an expression of the stream of your consciousness. You can go back and make corrections after you are finished, if you wish.

To derive maximum benefit, make it a habit and do it daily. However busy you may be, you can find fifteen minutes for this exercise on any day. You can write even when you are sick. Keeping your writing private is important so you can feel safe in expressing yourself freely.

I first learned about free writing in 1983 when I attended a workshop by Peter Elbow at Stony Brook University. I started to free write for fifteen minutes daily in my journal and continued the practice for about ten years. My thoughts became more and more crystallized in the process, and I was able to develop other formats for my writing. I still practice free writing but not every day.

After you have been writing for a couple of months and go back to read what you wrote, you will discover patterns in your thinking you were not aware of. You get to know yourself better. Spiritual growth is in knowing yourself more and more.

Writing every day, even for a few minutes, results in a consolidation of our thoughts. We become more centered and less scattered.

When we get in the habit of writing regularly, we discover that it is like meditation or prayer. It is another way of communicating with God. It can release stress and create peace. It can open your heart to new feelings and perceptions. You can ask questions and receive answers. You can find new perspectives on the conflicts in your life and experience healing. Through regular writing, you can discover new goals for yourself.

Writing is like any other skill in that it improves with practice. However, writing is different from many other skills in that it does not require special talent. Your life experience has enough rich material to write about. And through writing, you can find a much greater richness within yourself. Most well-known writers describe their own experiences in writing. And a lot of what they write is what they learned by writing.

Since your writing is private, you can express your feelings freely. You can write about your frustrations and your fears; you can write about your desires and about your dreams. It provides a non-judgmental space for you to express yourself and experience release, which leads to emotional healing. Most people carry residual memories of deep hurts experienced in early life which are, in many instances, forgotten by the conscious mind but continue to shape the patterns of our emotional responses. Such past experiences often reveal themselves in free writing. The writing process also often gives us a shift in perspective that contributes to the healing of old wounds.

In writing, you will find new insights and suggestions on what to do next. It provides you with direction and guidance. Author and film maker Julia Cameron writes in her book *The Right to Write:* "Over the years I have learned to 'go to the page' with questions regarding my work. I have asked for and received guidance on what to do next, on how to do better what it was that I was already doing. Posing the question, 'listening,' I often 'heard' answers that seemed to come from a source different from my normal consciousness. I would receive directives and advice that surprised me. Feeling resistance, but wanting to have an open mind, I would move out in faith on the suggested directions, only to find that the advice was sound and my work benefited. As a result of guidance, I wrote many things I otherwise would never have considered." This channel of guidance is available to everyone.

By writing about yourself and reading it over, you become an observer of yourself. You can see your life with detachment, a subject that you have described in words. You can then give good advice to yourself as you would give it to a friend.

To gain the advantages of writing, we have to engage in it. We have to release the belief that writing is only for people already known as "writers." You can write a few sentences now, and whenever you have a few minutes. You can write for fifteen minutes before going to bed, or the first thing in the morning, or during lunch break. You can write at your desk, at the kitchen table, or in bed. You can write at home or go to a cafeteria. No one is here to criticize what you write. You can choose to read or not read what you write. But as you build momentum and get into the habit, it will open new vistas and increase your power over life.

8

Expansion of Time

Sura 97 Ayas 2–4
And what will explain to you what the night of power is?
The night of power is greater than a thousand months.

According to the clock, there are twenty-four hours every day. However, we human beings experience time differently. When someone has nothing to do, a day seems to pass very slowly. But when he or she is engrossed in doing something, time goes quickly. On some days, we accomplish a lot in a few hours, while on other days, we accomplish little in the same amount of time. The clock shows the flow of time at a linear rate. For the human being, the experience of time is spiritual; it is nonlinear.

These verses are about the first experience of revelation by Prophet Muhammad. Ever since he was a young man, he was distressed by the backwardness of the society around him. With the passage of time, he became convinced that people's lives and behavior are related to their beliefs, and these have to change if society is to move forward. He went on many travels, met people with different religious beliefs, became pensive, and spent time in solitude looking for answers. In his thirties, he got in the habit of secluding himself for days at a time in a cave in the hills outside Mecca in contemplation. He concentrated his thoughts and he spoke words of worship and praise, day and night. Then one night it happened—the angel came and spoke five short sentences to him (which later became the first five verses of Sura 96). Everything changed that night. It is as if time had exploded. What the Prophet experienced that night was so momentous it could not have otherwise happened in thousands of months. The world was not going to be the same anymore. It was the night of power.

We human beings are thinking all the time. The thoughts of the majority of people are vague and scattered. They are looking at different objects and people around them and reacting. They say, this person looks friendly, that one is angry, this one has nice clothes, and that one is poorly dressed. It is hot today, it was raining yesterday. The mind jumps from one thought to another like a bird on a tree. There is no direction or objective. There is no accumulation of energy in their thoughts.

People who make a difference in the world are different. They have definite objectives. Such people always think about their goals. What should I do today to get to my objective? What have I learnt? Who can teach me how to get what I want? They avoid activities that hinder from their purpose. Their thoughts link to each other; they accumulate power. There may not be a visible change for a long time, but the unseen strength of their thoughts is gathering and collecting into a force. Then one day, a breakthrough occurs. They experience a huge change in a short time. It is as if time expanded. The progress you make in a few minutes, or a few hours, or a few days, is more than what was possible previously even in many years. You experience divine power flowing through you.

You have heard that you can achieve anything you want and whatever you desire can be yours. This is true, but it is possible only if you learn to fix your thoughts on your purpose. In order to achieve this, you have to let go of distractions; you have to prevent your mind from going to what you don't want. You have to stop looking at things that do not concern you; you have to get rid of the many pursuits that are interesting but diverge from your main purpose.

If you have small goals, you can obtain them by using your willpower. In order to experience an explosion of time, it is important to have unrealistic goals. You have to desire for things that are out of your present range. You have to have a purpose that is so big that if you tell your family, they will laugh at you. You need obstacles that are worthy to be burned by the divine flame.

Prophet Muhammad experienced another great expansion twelve years later. This was the night journey. He went to the highest heaven and came back in a few hours. This event marked another tipping point in his life. Before the night journey, his life was all hardship and struggle but little outward success. But after the night journey, there was a rapid increase in the number of people who accepted his message. His power and influence grew and in a few years, his message prevailed over all of Arabia, and it continued to spread to other parts of the world even after his death.

You can collect a bunch of grass and set it on fire by using a piece of glass. Sunlight has heat energy. Without the piece of glass, this energy goes in different directions and is scattered without causing a fire. The glass focuses sunlight at a point. The heat accumulates, and after a while, the grass becomes so hot it catches fire. Your ambition is like the piece of glass. You can use it to focus the power in your thinking. As you think more and more about what you want to accomplish, there will eventually be a flash. For a long time, nothing will happen because not enough energy has collected. But after enough concentration a breakthrough will occur. You will receive in a few hours what you previously could not have achieved in years.

It is reported in the books of Hadith that when Prophet Muhammad was out on the street walking, he kept his eyes with a downward focus in front of him. He did not look at people and things out of idle curiosity. He kept his attention on his own thoughts, even when he was out in the street.

People have misunderstood the night of power. The common wisdom is that since the Prophet experienced the night of power on the 27th of Ramadan, everyone should stay awake and pray during the 27th night of Ramadan. If you just stay awake for a night without a purpose, nothing will happen except that you will feel tired the next day. But if you want to follow the example of Prophet Muhammad, you have to first figure out what the purpose of your life is. God has placed His spirit within you, and He has made you His substitute on the earth. So what are you going to do to carry out this mission? How is the world going to be different because of all the resources God has invested in you? Everyone has to find an answer to this question.

And then you have to concentrate your thoughts and your energy on your special mission. It will appear impossible at first, but as you think more and more about how to accomplish your mission, you will find answers, your power will gather momentum, and then one day, you will experience an explosion of energy. You will experience your own night of power.

9

The Essence of Religion

Sura 98 Ayas 4–5

And those to whom scripture was given did not become divided into sects until after evidence had come to them.
But they were enjoined nothing more than to worship God, be sincere in religion and be regular in prayer and give charity, for this is the essence of religion.

The Quran, the Hadith, and all other books of scripture in the world contain parables, stories, advice, and prescriptions on a large number of topics. People in ancient times derived detailed rules of social, moral, and economic living from scripture and mandated obedience to these rules as religion.This became the doctrine of Fundamentalism. Different people came up with different rules.In this way, schisms and sects were formed, and they have been the source of strife in human history ever since. These ayas point out that the requirements of religion are few: faith in God, prayer, and charity, with the condition that we be sincere.

These ayas, when they were revealed, described the schisms among the followers of earlier scriptures. However, the same dynamic later unfolded among Muslims.

Different religious groups have different ways of prayer, and they make it a point of contention and division. It is noteworthy the Quran speaks repeatedly about the importance of prayer but does not prescribe a formulation for it.

The second aya mentions sincerity in religion as essential. Pretense makes prayer, charity, and all other good things we do ineffective. When a community ordains religion as following a large number of rules, then pretense becomes commonplace because it is too difficult to follow many rules. You are motivated not by your conscience but by the desire to seek approval of your community.

Becoming sincere and honest poses the greatest challenge in a person's spiritual development. Duplicity is bred into us from childhood when we learn to pretend to do things to seek approval from our parents. We become adults, but the habit of living for social approval stays with us.

Parents have the difficult task of teaching good habits and values to their children, and at the same time, allowing them enough freedom so their ability to think on their own stays intact. Since this is a difficult balance to achieve, most people become adults with a gap between what they feel is right and what they have been programmed into believing is right. A person's spiritual journey is the struggle to fill this gap. We become sincere when we realize on our own the value in traits of good character such as honesty, fairness, patience, and humility. We then try to live sincerely by these values. Our prayers and our works of charity then also become authentic and sincere.

Detailed rules of social life presented as religion did not emerge among Muslims until the great imams, more than a century after Prophet Muhammad. In the decades after the Prophet, the very few written copies of the Quran were not accessible to most people and there were no books of Hadith. *Fiqh,* or jurisprudence, had not yet been created as a system. The Muslim men and women of those days experienced religion through passages of the Quran and some Hadith they heard from others and had memorized. It is inspiration from these, and reasoning based on these, that guided the lives of Muslims. It was an era of great dynamism among Muslims.

A century later, Islam had spread to much of the known world among people with diverse cultures and languages. At that time, several scholars codified rules of sharia. These are rules to regulate all aspects of life, including how to wash yourself, what to eat and how to eat, conditions under which a woman could go out of the house, rules for borrowing and trading, the penal code, dress codes for women and men, rules for facial hair, how you should greet a non-Muslim, and myriad other rules, and these were all perceived as the unchanging religion. The different sets of rules prescribed by different imams led to the formation of sects, as this aya predicts.

As a result, a long era of conformity began which resulted in stagnation of Muslim social and spiritual life. In the centuries since then, Muslims have sought redemption in obeying rules they don't understand or question. The freezing of thought manifested soon in a demise of social, scientific, and artistic innovation. The Muslim world found itself in increasing isolation from progress that was being made elsewhere.

In order to benefit from spiritual teachings, it is important to separate the essential from the peripheral. We should recognize the principle of progressive change in religious as well as in cultural and social life. Truth is eternal, but the way it is expressed changes with time, and it is experienced differently by different people.

10

Every Little Thing Counts

Sura 99 Ayas 7–8
Anyone who does an atom's weight of good will see it,
And anyone who does an atom's weight of harm will see it.

These ayas point to the atomicity of life. Just as a castle is built by placing one brick next to another, life comes to us one moment after another. Each moment is brief, and it offers us choices. If you and I do something good in this moment, it will create goodness in the future. If we do something that harms us or someone else, it will produce its fruit in due time. What we will do at a given time is a small step, and therefore, it is easy to control. The many small steps we take over time link up to create our destinies.

Many times people are overwhelmed thinking that something big has to happen to change their life around. These ayas remind us of the power of taking small steps. Make a list of the many things you can do today. Decide on one item that is good for you that you know you can do. Then do it. However weak or off-track a person may be, he or she is usually strong enough to take one step in the right direction. The next day will offer this opportunity again. Everything we say or do makes a difference, and it accumulates. The opportunity to make a better future is in the small steps we take hour by hour and day by day.

Everyone knows that whatever we give out comes back to us multiplied. But many people get caught up in the feeling that they have so many expenses they cannot spare anything to give to charity. They say to themselves, "I will give when I have more money." By such thinking, they block the flow of abundance toward themselves. Prophet Muhammad said, *"Give in charity even if only half a date."* We should always be in the mode of giving, whatever our circumstances. On another occasion, the Prophet said, *"Removing an obstacle from the road is charity, and welcoming someone with a smile is also charity."*

The exchange of greetings with family, friends, acquaintances, or business colleagues may appear to be a small thing, but the enthusiasm with which we greet a person makes a difference in our relationship with him or her. Thus, it is said in Sura 4 Aya 86, *"When someone greets you with a greeting, reply with an even better greeting, or at least similar. Verily, God keeps account of all things. "*

The insight in these ayas is key to breaking the power of being overwhelmed. Many people are in a condition where they are burdened by so many duties and responsibilities that they do not have time to do what is really important for them. Thus, there are people who spend so much time working that they have little time to relax, to exercise, to be with the family, to read, or to pray. If someone stays on this track for a long time, their life goes out of balance. Although they may have success in their career, they will have deficits in their personal, social, and spiritual lives.

A solution to this type of overwhelm is in utilizing small snippets of time to create balance. If you don't have time to exercise, perhaps instead of taking the elevator, you can take the stairs, and you can climb two steps at a time. If you wish to read important books but don't have time, you can read just one page a day. In a year, you would have read a complete book. Some people want to read the Quran but find it difficult to understand. But you can read one aya and think about it until its meaning becomes clear. If you don't have time for prayer, perhaps you can count a few of your blessings and give thanks for them while you are riding on the bus.

The small steps link up and create a direction. Whenever we do something, it leaves a mark. If we do it again, the mark gets deeper, and if we keep repeating it, the mark becomes a groove. The groove then expands into a channel, the flow of which carries us to where we want to go.

The ease in taking small steps is of great value when we have a big project. It is important to first take the time to break the task into many small parts. Then we can do the work one easy step at a time. If you believe your child's college education is going to be very expensive, you can think ahead and save a small amount for this purpose each month. If you have to write a long report and thinking about it is making you stressful, you can first make an outline noting what different sections it will be made of, then divide each section into small segments. After that, just write one small segment at a time. This will make it much easier to write the report.

Some people have the opposite problem. They have free time, and they don't know what to do with it. They are bored. So they kill time by watching television, talking to their friends about nothing in particular, visiting stores, or playing cards. Many housewives are in such a situation. Most in this condition wish they could do something worthwhile, but feel they can't. Years of lethargy have sapped their self-confidence. People in such a situation also benefit by taking on small tasks that are of interest to them, such as doing volunteer work for half a day during the week, taking one class in a college, or joining a book club. If someone tries several activities, one at a time, they will sooner or later find something they are attracted to; their involvement can increase, and that will lead them to make a meaningful contribution.

Anything we think, say, and do is never lost. It accumulates. Thus, small acts of goodness or service, in reality, are seeds that sprout into much larger consequences. *Whatever of good you do beforehand for yourself, you will indeed find it with God—better and richer in reward* (Sura 73 Aya 20).

You can change your thinking patterns once you realize that thoughts occur in your mind one at a time. When you have a negative thought, you can pause and supersede it with a positive thought. For example, if the thought occurs to you, "I had a terrible childhood," you can pause and say something encouraging to yourself like, "But that was a long time ago. I am an adult now, and with the help of God, I can have a bright future." It takes only a few seconds. Replacing one thought by a better one is not difficult. If you get one negative thought removed from your thinking, it will be easier to remove another.

When we hear that someone has an unfortunate experience such as breakup of a family, failure in business, or someone is diagnosed with a serious illness, we often look for visible clues as to why it happened. But usually it is not a dramatic trigger but the sum of small atoms of harm the person has absorbed over time. For example, if you have a quarrel with someone once or twice a week, this adds up to a lot of quarrels over twenty years. Each has released toxins in your body and soul and the effects will come to the surface one way or another.

When a nation is subjected to attack, occupation, or humiliation, analysts and commentators often focus on some immediate visible cause as to why it happened. In reality, a community or a nation becomes weak gradually by the daily practice of unfairness, corruption, cruelty, and laziness by the individuals in its population over a long period of time.

Anyone who does an atom's weight of good will see it,
And anyone who does an atom's weight of harm will see it.

11

The Obsession for More and More

Sura 102

The obsession for more and more diverts you until you go to the graves.

But you will soon know, and again, you will soon get to know.

If you but knew it with certain knowledge you would be seeing a blaze.

Surely you will then see it with certainty of sight.

Then on that day you will be questioned about your indulgences.

The obsession for more and more wealth, fame, and fortune diverts us from knowing the possibility that life can have a higher purpose. We can do more than live for our whims. In the majority of people, the drive for acquisition continues until a person becomes certain of his or her death. This sura teaches us to become conscious of the value of life *now* so we can use our time for better purposes.

Deep meaning and fulfillment in life are obtained by working toward a purpose that is larger than yourself, something that creates goodness beyond our personal needs.

What your life's purpose can be depends on who you are. Everyone has a different disposition and different talent. For some, it is helping the poor; for others, it is removing injustice; for some others, it is creating new knowledge or new works of art. It can be dedicating yourself to raising good children, teaching wisdom, enabling people to live better, building a shelter for stray dogs and cats, or restoring the environment, or any other way in which we can serve God by serving His creatures.

The path to bliss begins by figuring out what purpose you are going to serve. What is it in your personality that when systematically applied can make the world a much better place? This requires you to think about yourself, about what will give you great satisfaction when you do it. But discerning your ideals and following through on them is not easy because our minds are clouded by obsessions rooted in our egos. We are already on a treadmill of interlocked demands that consume all our energies, leaving little room for thinking about a higher purpose. The crux of finding spiritual freedom is to loosen the grip of self-absorption, inferior motivations, and laziness that drains life away. We need all the discipline we can muster, and God's help, in changing direction so that instead of serving our weaknesses, we serve a higher purpose. That is why we say in Al-Fateha, "*We seek Your help so we can serve only You.*"

Prophet Muhammad said people do not appreciate what they can do with five assets before they are taken away by five calamities. People have a tendency not to appreciate health before becoming seriously ill, their wealth before it is squandered away, the energy of youth before it is replaced by the weakness of old age, the value of free time before it is replaced by preoccupation, and the opportunity of life before death overtakes them.

Many are caught up in obsessive pursuits of career success as if nothing else matters. There is no time to think about the meaning of life, to remember God, to talk to your wife or children, or even to take care of your health.

The obsession for more and fancier clothes, shoes, jewelry, furniture, houses, and cars diverts many people from realizing that there can be better uses for their money. The joy of things is so intoxicating for many people that the best use of free time they can think of is to go shopping. They don't know that self-esteem comes from internal attitudes and not from what you own.

The obsession of more and more varieties of foods and tastes diverts many from realizing that excessive eating is a waste of resources and bad for health. The zeal of gluttony traps people into habits that make them sick and die prematurely. People spend hours and hours cooking elaborate meals because they have not figured out a better use of their time.

The obsession for sex makes men spend time looking at women, fantasizing about them, and indulging in pornography. This passion diverts them from the reality that there is limited time and energy to do something worthwhile in life. The obsession is so deep that a lesson people learn in business school is that if you make advertisements with the image of any product juxtaposed with images of women, men will buy the product whether they need it or not.

But you will soon know, and again, you will soon get to know.
If you but knew it with certain knowledge you would be seeing a blaze.

It is a very useful spiritual practice to spend time with people who are terminally ill, those who have been told by doctors that nothing more can be done for them. They are now sure death is coming. It is no longer an abstract possibility. Instead, they see it with the eye of certainty. The priorities of a terminal person become rearranged quickly. The pleasures that occupied them until yesterday become unattractive. The years and years of struggling for things are reduced to ashes, as if consumed by a blaze. You cherish only the good things you were able to do, when you helped somebody, or you loved someone unselfishly.

Then on that day you will be questioned about your indulgences

The questioning is done by your Self. The spell of wayward desires is broken and the spirit comes to the surface to ask why you spent so much time in meaningless pleasures. What happened to all the money you had? How much was invested in good causes and how much was wasted?

An animal had to be killed to provide for your every meal. Many people worked to grow the grain you consumed, to transport it, to grind it, and cook it so you could eat it. You sucked up so many resources from the earth, and what did you contribute in return?

The universe works with the law of compensation. If you

borrow more and return less, you become a despised person. If someone does you a favor, you have to do a greater favor in return if you are an honorable person. The same law applies to the totality of our lives. We have to do our best to give more to the world than we consume in order to live here; only then do we deserve a house in heaven. If someone takes and takes and does not give back, then his life is like a pile of dry leaves to be consumed by fire.

You can own so many items that you have little time to do anything worthwhile. Your time and energy is taken up by thinking about your possessions, maintaining them, cleaning and polishing them, ordering parts for them, having them painted, moving them around, and showing them to your friends. This can take over your life.

But surely the opposite extreme of not owning anything and being poor is not the answer. If we are deprived and weak, we cannot make a contribution, and others have to take care of us. Moreover, the talent and genius that are gifted to every human being are not released in a state of helplessness and poverty.

There is a happy medium between self-deprivation and excess. We all need money and objects to live, to nurture ourselves and others, and to pursue our objectives. It is easy to understand the difference with the example of food. We need food to survive; we need food to be healthy and strong. We can and ought to choose between food that is beneficial and that is harmful. However, we can be so enamored with food that we regularly overeat. We can eat to while away time. Tastes can seduce our senses so we spend more and more time and resources to go after fancy foods. We can make food a matter of social prestige, and we can hold banquets to impress people. These are categories of desire that divert us from a higher purpose. Similar criteria for deciding between necessity and excess apply to all types of goods.

Once you discover within yourself how you want to service the world, your task then is to steer the ship of your life so you do embark on your purpose. You have to make plans and act on them. You have to let go of inferior pursuits. You ask for God's help for the success of your mission. This is what Prophet Muhammad did. This is also what every hero or heroine you have heard of did. You are the hero of your life. The only way to find lasting fulfillment is make your life the journey of a hero. You will then discover that what is in you is far greater than what you own and what you ever thought possible.

12

Law of Entropy

Sura 103
By the passage of Time,
Verily, man is in loss,
Except those who develop faith, and do good deeds,
And join together in the mutual teaching of Truth,
And of patience and constancy.

In physics, the law of entropy is known. It says that disorder increases in a system with time unless you supply energy to it.

If you roll a ball on the floor, it will not be able to continue going straight. The friction from the floor will make it wobble, and in time, the ball will change direction and eventually stop.

Life on earth is maintained because the sun sends energy into it. Without the flux of energy from the outside, the earth will freeze and all life on it will end.

Suppose you buy a piece of land and leave it unattended. In a few days, weeds will start growing. Passersby will throw garbage in it. Rats and snakes will come to live there. With the passage of time, it will become an ugly and dangerous place. For this piece of land to be neat and beautiful, you have to work regularly on its upkeep.

In any system, the passage of time creates deterioration unless there is an input of effort or energy. This sura points out that the law of entropy applies to human life also:

By the passage of Time,
Verily, man is in loss,

Your life is going to come apart with time unless you energetically embrace the principles of faith. We can observe this in the people we know. While most young people are dreaming of achieving great things, most old people live with regret. For the majority past a certain age, life appears like a no-win struggle. Many failed in the search for career success, wealth, fame, and love. Those who won some trophies find that the glitter goes away after a while. The children were so adorable when little but have grown up to cause you unhappiness. Henry Thoreau expressed this condition in his famous statement: "The mass of men lead lives of quiet desperation. What is called resignation is confirmed desperation; a stereotyped but unconscious despair is concealed even under what are called the games and amusements of mankind."

This sura provides a prescription for avoiding this fate. It says that people lose in life:

Except those who develop faith, and do good deeds
And join together in the mutual teaching of Truth,
And of patience and constancy.

Many times people talk about faith in complex theological language. But no matter which philosophy of faith we like, the bottom line is that positive faith is manifested in "good deeds," that is, in benevolence toward the world.

A small child experiences the world mostly in a self-centered manner: he feels that the role of others is primarily to meet his needs and desires. As we grow emotionally and spiritually, we can begin to grasp the notion that making contributions that go beyond our survival instincts gives us lasting meaning and satisfaction. Faith is, thus, obtained gradually.

There are many adults who have not grown beyond childish self-absorption. They live primarily for themselves, and in this way, fulfillment escapes them. They are unable to overcome feelings of jealousy, fear, and desperation. They wonder why in spite of hard work and the many things they acquired, they do not feel happy. Only through growth of our awareness that others are like us and a conviction to share the fruits of our talents with them can we find deep happiness and meaning. Confucius expressed this concept by saying, "The man of virtue, wishing to be established himself, seeks also to establish others; wishing to be enlarged himself, he seeks also to enlarge others."

In order to benefit from this teaching, we need to orient our short- and long-term goals so that they benefit not only ourselves but also others. We can choose to leave home every day with the intention of making a positive difference where we go and in what we do. And when we come back home, we can choose to enter with the intention of making a positive difference in the lives of those who live with us.

And join together in the mutual teaching of Truth,

Progress in faith is not automatic. Our thinking is molded by the people we meet regularly. The human mind is very malleable. The company we keep has a decisive impact on the direction of our lives.

The word "Truth" represents profound knowledge. Insight beyond the superficial is not obtained casually. Most of us get introduced to religion in childhood. The meanings and interpretations we have are derived from what our parents and teachers told us. In order to grow beyond childhood conditioning, we need to find the company of those who are seeking wisdom, and we need to form bonds such that we support each other in this quest. Such company is not only invaluable, but is also not easily available. People unaware of this insight do not make an effort to choose their society. Instead, they spend time with whoever is conveniently available and, thus, absorb attitudes and beliefs from random collections of people, and this builds an uncertain path for their future.

And of patience and constancy

Centering yourself in faith is a process. It requires giving up false beliefs and the lifestyle that goes with it. It is essential to be in the company of friends who are patient and encouraging when we falter and rejoice when we succeed, not the company of those who are critical of our efforts and jealous when they see us grow.

As you grow in faith, you become more and more optimistic, cheerful, and positive. You gain an inner conviction in the benevolence of God and the world He created. You feel grateful for who you are and know that all is well with you. It becomes easy for you to be good to others. This faith manifests in the happiness you find in your life, in your relationships, in your work, and in your own sense of well-being.

13

Mindless Prayer

Some of the questions often asked about prayer are: What is the purpose of prayer? Does it really work? Why can't I concentrate in prayer? Will I burn in hell if I don't pray?

We can get some answers by considering negative prayer, the prayer that harms. This is highlighted in Sura 107 Ayas 4–5:

There is calamity for those who are praying,
Who are unmindful in their prayer.

The practice of mindless prayer is very common. You are praying and your mind is somewhere else. It damages a person's spirit and produces chaos in his or her life. It is because of a lack of understanding of this fact that so many people who pray regularly live failed lives. Many others see them then conclude that it is better to stay away from religion.

How is calamity produced by prayer? To understand this, we should pay attention to the nature of communication.

You form an idea in your mind. You choose words to convey what you want to express. You then utter these words for the other person to understand. What happens if the words you speak do not represent what you are thinking inside? What is the impact if you are speaking, but your mind is somewhere else? What is the consequence if you speak words you don't even understand? This is miscommunication and lack of respect for the one you are speaking to. If you keep speaking like this, your relationship will break down.

God says in Sura 2 Aya 186:

If My servants ask you about Me—behold, I am near;
I respond to the call of him or her who calls.

Thus, when a person says something, there is always a response from God, but it is a *response*; it reflects and amplifies what is in your call. If your state of mind during prayer was hope, the response will fulfill the hope; if your state of mind was confusion, the response from God will bring confusion in your life.

An analogy for prayer is a musician playing the guitar in front of a large audience. The musician plucks on the strings and the powerful sound system amplifies the vibrations of his fingers to the audience. The movement of his fingers conveys his feelings to the strings. These are then amplified and distributed everywhere and the audience reacts accordingly. Similarly, when you pray, you convey your feelings to God. In this analogy, God is like the sound system that amplifies what you say and distributes it everywhere. The world is then moved to bring you experiences that contain the feelings you conveyed in your prayer.

Many who pray prescribed prayers out of fear convey this emotion, and the response from God creates situations of fear for them. Many pray with words that are meaningless for them; and the reward for them is a meaningless life. Many feel guilty that they are not diligent in their observance; their life is filled with guilt and remorse.

The importance of regular prayer is emphasized repeatedly in the Quran. Prayer, or *salat*, is the essence of faith. It is the primary path to God-consciousness. However, a remarkable fact is that the Quran does not recommend a format for prayer. The Quran insists that people should pray but consistently avoids prescribing a method for doing it. The reason is that the Quran does not see Muslims as a separate group who pray in a particular way. In the Quran, a Muslim is anyone who has faith in God. It speaks of all humanity and the universal truths that relate man to God.

It is a tragedy of massive proportions that teachings in the Muslim tradition evolved to take a totally opposite view. Adherence to format is considered an absolute must for prayer. People are made to memorize the Arabic words, the correct pronunciation, the body postures and their sequences, with frequent reminders that any departure from the prescribed routine makes the prayer defective and unacceptable to God. People are told that it may be better for them to know the meaning of the words, but it is not necessary; what matters is that you utter the words with correct Arabic pronunciation.

The central important fact that your innermost thoughts and feelings are the essence of prayer is missing. There is seldom a discussion of the depth of meaning, of hope and expectation, of creating a lofty purpose for your life, and prayer a means of achieving it. Instead, the format of prayer has become the purpose.

With absence of meaning and purpose, people, when praying, often find their attention wandering everywhere. They experience boredom, frustration, dejection. They also experience guilt for feeling like this. These are the emotions they convey to God in their prayers day after day and month after month. They then find boredom, frustration, dejection and guilt dominating their lives.

This emphasis on outward correctness has now been programmed into Muslims for so many generations that prayer is commonly described as an "obligation." The idea that prayer could be spontaneous or joyful is almost heretical. If you frequent a mosque, any mosque, you will get to know some of the people who are very particular about prescribed prayer. They come to attend the service several times a day and have been doing so for many years. They are committed to ritual prayers they don't understand. As you get to know them, you will find, inevitably, that these people have become mindless in their attitudes, they are confused and uninformed, pessimistic and purposeless. They are unable to understand simple things but are quick to take issue and get into an argument. These are living testimonials to the Ayas (107:4–5):

There is calamity for those who are praying,
Who are unmindful in their prayer.

Repeated prayer is very powerful, but it is a sword with two edges. If you learn to use it properly, it can help you create a life of great power and effectiveness. It will help you fulfill your dreams. On the other hand, if you don't use it properly, it will cut your life to pieces.

Because prayer is so powerful, you have to first spend time—a lot of time—to understand it. There is no shortcut in learning an instrument of power.

The first step in spiritual growth is to create a time every day when you can be by yourself to think and reflect; a time in which you can be detached from the humdrum of life so you can be aware of the thoughts and feelings that are circulating in you. Prophet Muhammad said that *an hour of introspection is better than a year of prayer.*

The words of prayer you already know have sublime meanings. Think of these meanings and how they relate to your life. The words of prayer, any prayer, contain feelings of compassion, gratitude, caring, contentment, peace, optimism, expectation, enthusiasm, joy, responsibility, service, and purpose. Train yourself to say the words of prayer such that the feelings in them come alive when you say them. Find a teacher or a friend who can help you in this. With practice, the quality of this experience will improve. There will be positive changes in you. Your prayer will evolve. The good feelings when they are strong enough will urge you to pray more. In this way, you can grow directed by your own inner experience toward better and more effective prayer, and its manifestation in the world.

14

Lack of Faith

The ayas about mindless prayer in the previous chapter are part of a statement of symptoms of deficient faith that makes up Sura 107:

Do you see the one who is in denial of the law of compensation?
Such a one who rebuffs the orphan,
And does not encourage feeding the downtrodden.
There is calamity for those who are praying,
Who are unmindful in their prayer.
Those who do things for the sake of appearance,
And avoid doing simple acts of kindness.

These traits are found in all of us to some extent because faith is obtained through a process of growth. An infant's awareness of the world is limited to the few people around him, and he sees them primarily as tools to fulfill his needs. As we grow and mature, we become more aware that other people have needs, too, and we should help them. But the traits of self-absorption stay in us, more in some and less in others. Some of these traits are listed in this sura. The journey of spiritual growth consists of moving away from self-centeredness toward awareness that we are connected to everyone and we are connected to God.

Do you see the one who is in denial of the law of compensation?

The law of compensation is that everything we do has a consequence. What we say has a consequence, how we say it has a consequence; what we do has a consequence, how we do it has a consequence; what we do to others comes back to us sooner or later. Nothing we do is meaningless or small. If you are cruel to a cat, you will suffer for it. If you give water to a thirsty dog, you will be rewarded for it. In everything we are doing, we connect with the heavens through our intentions. At any given time, I am either a source of good receiving good or I am a source of evil receiving evil. Faith is knowing that the law of compensation is real and then learning to take control of what we say and do.

Such a one who rebuffs the orphan

In the Arab culture in which these ayas were revealed, a person's status was determined by the power of his or her family. The orphan was without power or influence. The orphan, therefore, symbolizes a helpless person, someone whom no one backs or protects. A person lacking in faith is often contemptuous of those who need help. There is no visible cost to him for deriding or rebuffing such a person.

But the law works the same for everyone. If you or I insult a weak person, there will be adverse consequences for us, even though that individual cannot defend himself.

And does not encourage feeding the downtrodden

Note the aya does not say, "does not feed the downtrodden." Instead, it says "does not *encourage* feeding the downtrodden." It is not good enough to make a donation and say, "I did my part." This aya asks us to become activists in helping those in need. The benefits of helping others are so vast that to live a self-centered life with only token help for others is a sign of defective faith.

While the aya speaks of feeding the hungry because food was scarce in the Arabian desert when this aya was revealed, the weak and the disadvantaged today need help with not only food, but in many other categories, such as shelter, health, economic development, and knowledge. This aya defines a person of faith as someone who is proactive in organizing and orchestrating help for the disadvantaged. In order to respond to this teaching, we must reorient our lives and our careers such that we devote ourselves to the service of others.

There is calamity for those who are praying,
Who are unmindful in their prayer.

In prayer, a person is speaking to God, the Almighty. Praying while you are thinking of something else is taking God's name in vain; it is disrespectful. Similarly, speaking words you don't understand, or not paying attention to what you say, is unmindful prayer.

People think inattentive prayer is acceptable because they see others pray the same way. If a person prays in a mindless manner, it means he thinks what he says to God does not matter. This is deficient faith. In reality, what we say to God is the most important communication. You have to think about it carefully, prepare for it, and be fully aware when you are saying it.

Mindful prayer is not easily acquired. You have to train yourself to calm the swirl of random thoughts and pictures that are in your brain. You have to pause and feel each word. It takes dedication and practice.

Inattentive prayer often arises because the person is trying to conform to a tradition or a social expectation. Your heart is not in it, but you feel you must pray because it is expected of you; you are keeping up appearances, a character flaw discussed next.

Those who do things for the sake of appearance

All of us started our lives as little children when we knew our happiness depended on seeking the approval of our parents. They knew what was best, and we should think and speak the way that pleased them. And when we wanted to do something different, we pretended. We did what they wanted us to do for the sake of appearance.

But we can still be stuck in the same mode, even after we become adults. It is not easy to switch habits quickly. Some people continue to live to please their parents. Others replace the parents with other authority figures they obey. It can be a boss, a spouse, your extended family, a religious figure, or your ethnic group. You conduct yourself to *appear* good, so they would look at you approvingly. You are living as a slave to others. It is a neurotic condition.

In societies where conformity is insisted upon, many people grow up so addicted to approval they have little initiative in adult life. You can be so dependent on authority figures you are unable to know your own will. You end up in a career others choose for you, you get married to someone others choose for you, you live in a house others choose for you, and you say prayers others choose for you.

Living for the sake of appearance is the ultimate loss. You had only one life to live, and you gave it away to please others. You did not use this opportunity to discover what makes you special and different. You did not appreciate that your uniqueness is God's gift to the world. You did not muster the strength to nurture your talents and to express them to create joy for yourself and for the world.

And avoid doing simple acts of kindness

Everyone has opportunities several times a day for being helpful, for doing simple acts of kindness. If we greet people with a smile, are cheerful in demeanor, are willing to stop and give directions to someone who asks, make room for another person, give our seat to an elderly person on a bus, loan something we are not using to someone who wants it, and speak well of others, we add civility to our surroundings and our own well-being increases. Faith teaches us that the way we are toward others is the way the world will be toward us.

It is easy to do simple acts of kindness if we are feeling good inside. If, on the other hand, your mind is filled with the demons of negativity, you feel awful and you are not inclined to be kind. People who feel they have been wronged are filled with images of anger, resentment, or self-pity, and often, they project these feelings on everyone they meet. People who feel what they have is too little are unwilling to do even small favors for others. Such states of mind represent a lack of faith.

Progress in faith begins with becoming aware of the thoughts that flow in our minds. It is then adopting the view that God has created you for a positive purpose, God loves you, and the life given to you is a gift. It may not seem like this by looking at what is going on in your life right now, but you choose this belief. God has a grand plan for your life. The troubles you are having are part of the plan. Any hero or heroine has to go through tough situations before he or she becomes victorious, and you have a similar journey. Within you He has stored resources which are more than enough to overcome your difficulties and make a great life which will be a joy for you as well as for others. So why not start acting like that now?

The purpose of prayer is to convey this perspective of faith to us. Conscious, deliberate, and repeated prayer makes us gradually understand and internalize the insights of faith. Our internal states become happier. Fear is replaced by hope, and it becomes easier to be kind to others. As faith takes root in us, we feel joy in helping others. The more proactive we become in service to others, the more goodness we receive, and our life becomes an upward spiral.

15

Abundance

Sura 108
Behold, I have granted you abundance.
Be mindful of the Lord who nurtures,
And sacrifice.
Verily, the opposition to you will be cut off.

The teaching in this sura is very brief but also very powerful. It contains the secret to life. But because of its few words, it has been misunderstood by many. People read it and say, "How can it be that God has given us abundance? I am poor and miserable. There is no abundance. The aya says, 'I have given you abundance,' but I don't see it, so there must be another meaning." There are so many unhappy people. How can it be that God has given abundance to human beings? So people have come up with another explanation. They say abundance has been given to Prophet Muhammad, not to anyone else. It is a special gift to the Prophet because God loved him so much. So we should pay special homage to the Prophet because of the great honor he received.

By this kind of superficiality, the meaning has been missed. Instead of seeing and utilizing the universal meaning in the ayas, many people turned their religion into a worship of the Prophet. The Quran says Muhammad is a human being just like everyone, but many of his followers don't believe it. They have placed him on a special pedestal and spend their time glorifying him, not learning from his example, but singing hymns about him.

Creation of the human being is described in Sura 32 Aya 9 in these words, *He made him complete and breathed into him of His spirit.* Because of the power of the divine spirit in the human being, he creates everything in abundance, in profusion, in plenty, compared to the other species with whom he shares this planet. And this ability comes from our ability to focus our attention. We human beings have the ability to think, and we shape the world with our thinking. What we think continuously, what we imagine, what we talk about again and again, we find in great abundance. Let us consider some examples:

Home is a place of rest and shelter. Every species makes a home. A bird makes a home in a tree, and a fox makes its home in a cave. But a human being makes his home a place of abundance and excess. One or two people make a house of five or six rooms, and even ten or twenty rooms. People's homes have to be painted and lighted and filled with furnishings for comfort and decoration. This is an example of the human being's ability to create abundance.

A squirrel or a deer searches for food and can find what is needed for its survival. But the human being creates foods of hundreds of varieties and tastes, not because they are needed for his survival, but because he manifests abundance.

Two animals in a forest can become hostile and fight. But they will fight for a short time, then one will decide to run away and the other becomes the winner. But when human beings become hostile, they assemble armies equipped with deadly weapons and kill thousands of each other, and keep fighting for years. This is an example of man creating an abundance of destruction.

These examples can be multiplied in every aspect of life. Humans create everything in great excess. We create prosperity, comfort, knowledge, beauty, and well-being in great excess. We also create misery, conflict, destruction, and ugliness in great abundance. That is why it is said, *"We created man of a most excellent fabric, then We rendered him the vilest of the vile"* (Sura 95 Ayas 4–5).

This is how some people become highly educated, or establish successful businesses, or create a happy home, or excel in music, or in sports, or become skillful writers, or amass great wealth, or get close to God, or achieve whatever they choose as the object of their focus.

Negative abundance is achieved by people who are persistently thinking about their misfortune. Their minds are concentrated on what is making them unhappy. They look for reasons to complain. This creates a life of great unhappiness.

There are people whose lives result in nothing. They think of nothing in particular. Their desires are weak, and their attention wanders from object to object. Such a person's mind is like a monkey in the forest. It sits on a branch for a little while and then it jumps to another branch, and then another branch, and the day is over like this. The power of the spirit in them also creates but does not have the chance to accumulate. You can live for a long time and have nothing to show for it. You created nothingness in abundance.

After reminding us that He has given us abundance, God teaches us how abundance of good is to be found:

Behold, I have granted you abundance.
Be mindful of the Lord who nurtures,
And sacrifice.

Please pay attention how the second aya is constructed. God is speaking, but now He speaks of Himself in the third person, pointing to His attribute of nurture. He says, "Remember your *Rabb*, the Lord who nurtures you, supports you, and cherishes you."

The phrase I have translated as "*Be mindful of*" can also be translated as "*Be connected with*," or "*Pray to.*" Thus, the second aya can also be: "*Remain connected with the Lord who nurtures*," or "*Turn in prayer to the Lord who nurtures.*" Prayer is an effort to connect with the Almighty by bringing Him to your mind.

Thus, in order to receive an abundance of good, make your prayer a reminder that God nurtures you, is taking care of you, cherishes you. His power is unlimited, and you always have His help. You are never alone or abandoned. If you maintain this focus every day, what you ask for will emerge in great abundance.

Like everyone, you have dreams and desires. Pick one that is the most important to you. Think continuously about achieving it, day in and day out. Eliminate thoughts that conflict with your goal. Pray for what you want; ask how you can find what you are looking for; believe that God will bring about what you want; work on your plan; stay positive in the face of discouragement. Remember your *Rabb* who nurtures you. Soon, you will find ideas and people to help you fulfill your goal, and you will find it in great abundance.

In order to obtain abundance, we have to sacrifice by living a life of discipline. You have to give up distractions and concentrate your energy on your objective. Idle talk, gossip, and laziness have no room in the life of a person seeking something worthwhile. You have to make time daily to remember the nurture of your Lord.

You will find true abundance only if you seek it to help others. Your objective has to be a source of good for the world. We have to sacrifice our tendency to be selfish, to desire from the ego. In order to be connected to the Lord who nurtures, our objective has to be to nurture others.

Verily, the opposition to you will be cut off.

When abundance begins to manifest in a person's life, opposition will also appear. Those who are upset with your success will show up. If you get many promotions at work, or your business expands, or you become very knowledgeable, or you have a happy marriage, or your children are doing really well, some people will be there to sabotage you. Even people close to you or related to you can feel threatened by your abundance. This is because jealousy is a big part of human nature. As long as a person is weak and inconsequential, nobody notices. But when you begin to succeed, many will rise up to oppose you.

The sura teaches that the way to deal with the opposition is to remember your Lord who nurtures you. It is a mistake to be obsessed with those who oppose you. We should pay attention to the larger picture. The world is ruled by God, who helps those with the highest motives. If we stay focused on being a source of good, the abundance will accumulate for us and the opposition will be overcome. But if we fixate our attention on those who are opposing us, we will make them powerful in our minds, and they will be able to hurt us.

Prophet Muhammad has given a metaphor for the abundance God gave him. He said it is like a pond, the waters, of which, are drawn from a river in paradise. Those who will drink from it are blessed and will find entry into paradise. According to a Hadith, this river in which God has infused abundant good is sweeter than honey, whiter than milk, cooler than snow, and smoother than cream. Its banks are made of rubies, and the cups with which you drink are made of silver, and those who drink this water will never be thirsty again.

This is an allegorical description of the divine wisdom in the revelations the Prophet received. Those who understand it and use it will find good in great abundance.

16

Living in Reaction

Sura 11: Ayas 9–11

If We let man taste our grace and then take it away from him—behold, he abandons hope, forgetting all gratitude.

And if We let him taste our favor after trouble has visited him, he is sure to say, "Gone is all affliction from me!"—for behold, he enjoys boasting.

[Most people are like this] except those who are patient in adversity and do things that are right: it is they whom forgiveness of sins awaits, and a great reward.

The first two ayas describe the state of mind of people who do not see the divine rules of cause and effect. They tend to be reactive in their understanding of life. If something they like happens, they feel exultation and pride, but when painful situations occur they become dispirited and lose hope. These attitudes are contrary to faith and drain a person's power. By overcoming these patterns of thinking, we can tap into the full power of faith and raise our lives above the ordinary.

Hope is a cornerstone of faith. Everyone goes through difficult circumstances. Everyone has setbacks, tragedy, and loss. A person with faith knows that God is beneficent and merciful. This is the reason not to give up hope that his or her problems will be resolved and life will become better. They say, "I don't know what the way out is, but I know there is a way out, and I will find it with the help of God. I am sure some benefit will emerge from the troubles I have." A person of faith never says there is no use trying, never thinks that the situation is hopeless.

The second symptom of a weak faith mentioned here is being ungrateful in times of trouble. It is easy to feel happy and thankful when everything is going well. But it requires a strong faith to be thankful when things are not well. We should remember that being appreciative and thankful is a practice for making life better. No matter how bad the circumstances appear to be, there are some good things in your life that you can notice. If a person cannot see anything to be happy about in the present, they have happy memories. You can remember the favors you received in the past and feel happy about them. Just as you were happy sometime in the past, you can be happy again in the future. This is a reason to be happy about now and give thanks for.

The third advice in these ayas is not to be boastful when you find success. Surely it feels good to be proud, to think that your success is all about yourself and talk to everyone as such. But if you think, "I did it all by myself," then in your moments of weakness, you will feel alone and vulnerable. Moreover, boasting turns away good people. Only sycophants who want to take advantage of you stay, and your success becomes vulnerable to a sudden crash. A person who thinks that his accomplishment came about because of help from God and from people is anchored in a much-sounder belief that helps continued success. Why not believe that a power much greater than yourself is helping you? Why not believe that your life is part of God's plan to make the world into a better place? Why not eradicate fear of the future by acknowledging the help of God? It is wise to be humble before God. It is not wise to be puffed up and walk with a swagger.

The third aya speaks of people who have overcome these limitations and have developed a strong faith. Adversity does not thwart them. Faith protects them from becoming pessimistic or bitter. They continue to work toward their goals patiently. They do what is right. They know that good action leads to good results sooner or later.

It is a common misconception that if you are down on your luck, you have justification to act unethically. We hear people say, "My brother looses his temper easily these days. He yells at his wife and children because he has trouble in his business." We should know that excuses don't help. Every wrong action has its bad consequence that we must pay for sooner or later. A person of faith disciplines his or her emotions, or if they are beyond control, seeks professional help.

Also, people say that corruption is common in such-and-such a country because people are poor. They have no choice; if they don't steal, they are going to be hungry. This is reverse logic. People remain trapped in misfortune as long as they do not develop faith in goodness, until they learn to be patient in adversity, and make the best choices under all circumstances.

it is they whom forgiveness of sins awaits, and a great reward.

All of us have made mistakes. At different stages of our lives, we have acted against our better judgment. We have acted unethically and selfishly. These acts of sin have hurt us and limited our possibilities. But if we grow in faith, we remain steadfast in adversity, we keep doing the right thing day after day, we keep our composure even if we don't see progress, and stay hopeful, eventually, the deficit of our mistakes is paid up, and we experience breakthroughs in our capacities, and new vistas become open to us by the grace of God.

Another common weakness mentioned several times in the Quran is that when people have trouble, they pray earnestly, but when the trouble is gone and they are feeling good, they forget about God. Let us consider Sura 41 Aya 51:

When We bestow favors on man he turns away and keeps aloof [from Us]; but when misfortune touches him, he is frequent with prayers.

Similar meaning is found in Ayas 10:12; 16:53–55; 17:67; 29:65–66; 30:33–34; 31:32; 39:8.

We can see this every day. When people run into trouble, they turn to prayer. They appeal to God sincerely and earnestly. They have no difficulty in believing that God can help them. This can be seen when someone has a serious accident, or on an airplane when it is caught in turbulent air, in a family where there is serious illness, when someone has suffered a major loss of income, or where a child is a source of trouble in a family. But it is also commonly seen that people lose interest in prayer when their problem is resolved and they come into a happy condition, not knowing that their life would be so much better if they recognized that God is always present. It will help them if they cement their relationship with God when life is pleasant.

A person's relationship with God can be likened to a rope. Every time you think of God and call upon Him in a sincere manner, you add a strand to it. If you make it a practice to pray regularly, the rope keeps getting stronger, and eventually, you can feel it; it becomes a perceptible source of support for you in good times and bad. You can easily grasp it because it is always there. You no longer feel alone or feeble. But if you do not remember God for a long time, the strands unravel, one by one, and we no longer see the rope of God. So when bad times come again, we feel we are without support and fall into despair.

The way people pray when they are in trouble is very instructive. You can see the sincerity, the earnestness, and the emotion in the prayer. People pray as they are, sitting in a waiting room, standing in line or in a hospital bed. People pray when they are driving or cooking and when they wake up in the night. They do not need any special rituals or preparations for prayer. The need is urgent, and the heart cries out for help. Your mind does not wander and concentration is easy. These are the attitudes that make prayer effective. One of the many benefits of hardship is that it teaches us how to pray, so we can continue with it later when the trouble is removed from us.

17

Change Yourself if You Want to Change Your Circumstances

Sura 13 Ayas 9–11

He knows what is hidden and what is open; the Almighty, the Exalted.

It is the same whether any of you thinks quietly or speaks aloud and whether he is hidden by the night or is out in the day,

With each person there are forces behind him and ahead of him coming in succession: they preserve him at the behest of God.

Verily, God does not change people's condition unless they change their inner selves,

And when God causes people to suffer misfortune, there is no averting it, and they will not find any protector besides Him.

The thoughts we think within ourselves create the forces that surround us and drive our lives forward. What we are experiencing today is the result of what we have thought and said in the past. What we are thinking today will shape our future. In this way, God has placed control of everyone's destiny within his or her own mind. You are the only one thinking in your mind, and you are the only one who can speak through your mouth. These are the powers through which you express your beliefs, formulate your desires, and take action. God receives and assembles everything you and I put out and gives back to us conditions and circumstances in accord with our thoughts.

If you want to experience total freedom and live fully, you have to grasp the message of these ayas. You are the thinker, and God is the responder. You are in charge of your life; you can make what you want of it. You will make what you will by what you think in your mind day and night, when you are alone, and when you are with others.

With each person there are forces behind him and ahead of him coming in succession: they preserve him at the behest of God.

People are not aware of the power within them because they don't see the relationship between their thoughts and their circumstances. What you are thinking now seems to be inconsequential. You can say anything and nothing seems to happen. You can say, "I want to be happy," but the physical reality is that you have many things that make you unhappy. So you say to yourself, "What I think does not matter. The world and my luck have deprived me of happiness." You don't realize that you are thinking a thought every microsecond, so while one thought is like a little drop, what you think again and again and again for a long time gathers together to form the gigantic tide that pushes the ship of your life. Another factor to understand is that everyone has only a few thoughts they have again and again. When we are out and about talking with people, we think we talk of many different things, but within ourselves, each of us has two or three patterns of thinking through which we evaluate our lives. It is our persistent and repeated thoughts that shape our circumstances.

God protects us from the consequences of many of our foolish thoughts. His benevolence tilts the outcomes in our favor. Prophet Muhammad said that if someone thinks a thought of doing something good, he gets a reward just for thinking this thought. And if he follows through and does what he intended, then he gets ten or more rewards. If, on the other hand, someone thinks of doing something harmful, he is not punished for it. But if he follows through and does the bad deed, then one demerit is written into his account. In this way, we are protected from occasional negative thoughts that occur to us. Only if such thoughts are persistent in us and we follow through do we face the negative consequences.

Another favor of God in the way He has created the world is that there is often a delay between what we are thinking and its manifestation in our lives. This gives us human beings protection by creating a margin of safety for errors in our thinking. We can become wiser and change what we focus on before its results show up in our lives.

Verily, God does not change people's condition unless they change their inner selves

Everyone wants their condition to be better. Life has

brought us situations in which we are unhappy and we wish our lives could improve. These ayas point out that God will help change our life if we change what is in our *nafs,* in the deep part of us. The controls for changing our circumstances are not in what we see around us, but *within* us, in the invisible parts of us, where our thoughts, perceptions, and beliefs reside.

This is because in order to change anything, we have to take some action. But the action a person takes, or whether a person takes action or remains passive depends on what he or she thinks and feels. And our thoughts and feelings emerge out of our deeply held beliefs.

An important inference from this aya is that blaming does not help us. This includes blaming people, blaming circumstances, or blaming bad luck. This insight does not deny that other people are involved in making the difficulties we face; it says that blaming is not going to help. To make things better, we have to improve the way *we* think, how *we* look at the issues, the questions *we* ask, the assumptions *we* make about life.

We all know this to be true from experience. In every college, there are some students who blame the teachers for not teaching properly or who think that they are not doing well because the curriculum is bad. Such students usually end up at the bottom of the class. In the same school, there are other students who focus on their own habits. They try to discipline themselves and focus their time and energy on learning what is available. Such students usually emerge at the top of the class.

In the work environment, we see people who habitually blame their boss, the company, or their coworkers. Such people are usually unhappy in their work and do not get promoted. There are others in the same organization that stay away from backbiting and gossip. They focus on doing their work in the best possible way. No matter what the profession, such people often rise to positions of authority.

For six years, I volunteered as a marriage counselor in a large mosque. Soon after starting this work, I realized that, while every family is different, there is something common among the couples who have serious differences. They blame each other. The husband is convinced that their marriage is bad because of how the wife is, and the wife describes, again and again, how irresponsible or insensitive the husband is. On the other hand, if a husband can see that his life can be better if he changes the way he thinks about his wife, and the wife has a similar realization about her own thinking, then the relationship begins to heal quickly.

There are communities and nations in which poverty, disease, and powerlessness are present. The attitude of blame is pervasive in such communities. People are convinced they have troubles because other more powerful people are exploiting them. On the surface this is very likely to be true. But the way out is the advice in the aya: *"Verily, God does not change people's condition unless they change their inner selves."* In some nations, there is division and infighting. People often say they are fighting because others have conspired to divide them. In reality, no one can divide people unless feelings of enmity already existed within their *inner selves*. And they have the option of changing these thoughts anytime by replacing hatred with kindness and suspicion by trust.

Blaming others not only does not help us, it takes us in

the wrong direction. Every time you say someone is making your life difficult, you strengthen the belief that your life is controlled by others. The more you blame, the deeper this belief becomes in you. This belief then guides you to take actions that create more circumstances that verify your belief.

When you are facing a difficulty and the notion comes in your mind: "It is because of such-and-such a person, or my family, or because of the weather, or the economy, or the government," just let go of this thought. Say to yourself, "I think differently now. I can figure out how to solve this problem, and the help of God will come as I try." Whatever the nature of the problem we face, we can ask the question: "What can *I* do to make things better?"

The principles of morality that are universally accepted are based on the fact that each of us can create a better life for ourselves by changing ourselves. For example, no matter where I am in life, I can make it better by becoming more sincere and less duplicitous, by being more generous and less stingy, by thinking about others as I would like them to think about me.

The life story of Prophet Muhammad is an example of the principle outlined in these ayas. He was born in Arabia, a land without structures of civilization, with no schools, libraries, courts, or government. There were no resources except the few camels and sheep that could survive in the hot desert. In this barren milieu, Muhammad was born an orphan without an opportunity to learn to read or write. As a young man, he supported himself by tending sheep for people. There was plenty that he could feel angry or disgruntled about, but Muhammad did not choose that path. The revelations he received in subsequent years taught him how to change himself and others for the better. The Quran is the compendium of these revelations.

The Quran teaches us to change our inner selves by thinking thoughts of faith, of hope, gratitude, generosity, love, compassion, and taking responsibility for our lives. It wants us to believe that God is kind and merciful. He is near us, hears us, and responds to us. Prayer and *dzikr* are methods of inculcating these thoughts.

The Quran teaches us to change our inner selves by giving up thoughts of complaining, despair, ingratitude, anger, stinginess, dishonesty, and arrogance.

And when God causes people to suffer misfortune, there is no averting it, and they will not find any protector besides Him.

When people persist in the wrong way of thinking for a long time, when hopelessness, discord, and fear have depleted their ability to take positive action, then disaster has become inevitable. Calamity and suffering are from God because He has made the rule that what people think and say shape their circumstances. The misfortunes are from within ourselves and we can come out of them by changing how we think.

18

How to Change Your Inner Self

Sura 13 Aya 11

Verily, God does not change the condition of people unless they change their inner selves.

This aya describes the reality of how the world is and how we interact with it. The experiences we have in the world emanate from what we have inside of us, in our thoughts and feelings. The energy inside a human being is powerful; it flows outward and attracts people and objects with similar energy. If we want to reshape the conditions around us, we must learn to shape how we think and feel within us.

Note that the statement is in the negative: *God does not change the condition of people unless they change their inner selves.* The Quran expresses categorical truths with negative sentences. For example, instead of saying, "There is one God," it says, "*There is no deity except God.*"

The negative construction excludes all other possibilities. Similarly, by saying "*God does not change the condition of people unless they change their inner selves,*" it tells us that there is no possibility that our conditions can be changed if we focus our efforts only on what we see on the outside.

This aya also reveals an aspect of the nature of God. The power of God resides in your heart; it projects your thoughts and feelings outward and creates your circumstantial reality.

Those whose hearts have feelings that the world is a good place are guided to look for goodness and find it. Those who feel that people are unfair subconsciously draw to themselves people who treat them unfairly. Those who feel they have plenty of money find it easy to be generous and find that wealth comes to them. Those with persistent images of fear in their minds get into circumstances that cause more fear.

The main life issue this aya points to is this: We all have had experiences that have created emotional scars in us. Unless we heal these scars, their destructive force multiplies in us and creates the corresponding reality in our daily experience. In order to have a better life, we have to figure out ways to change how we feel inside.

People have painful experiences. Perhaps you were raised by abusive parents, or you came across bad teachers, or you placed trust in someone and they took advantage of you, or you were seriously injured in an accident, or you face prejudice because of who you are, or you have suffered serious illness, or your child is handicapped, or you did your best to raise your child, but he or she turned out to be irresponsible, or you went through a bitter divorce, or you were raped, or you worked hard to build a business and then lost it, or your town was attacked by an army and you had to flee to save your life, or you had other devastating experiences. What should we do with such memories? We can talk about our pain to others, and it sometimes brings relief. However, unless we systematically work to cure our negative feelings, repeated recounting of the painful occurrence hardens its image and makes it more real. The scar of the initial experience becomes bigger and overwhelms our perceptions. It can define who we are and lock us into its perpetual experience. There are people who have talked about their suffering so much that it defines who they are. It becomes the telescope through which they look at life and evaluate everything that happens.

For example, if we were taken advantage by someone, we can become locked into the belief that no one can be trusted. If we felt pain in the family we grew up in, we can come to believe that happiness is not possible in a family, etc.

The main spiritual challenge is to heal the scars that life has given us and turn them into springboards of happy and successful living. I.e., we have to learn to change our inner selves for the better.

Positive affirmations, or statements that we speak repeatedly, provide a powerful way of changing our inner selves.

The physical energy of the words we speak is felt inside us and is converted into spiritual energy. For example, all of us know that some things we say can make us feel encouraged while other words we say can make us feel discouraged.

Whether we are aware of this or not, all human beings use affirmations, that is, the statements they speak again and again. For example, in our present culture, people often say this related to their work: "Thank goodness it is Friday," and "I don't believe it is Monday morning again." Both convey the idea that your work is a chore you want to avoid. People in our culture also speak positive affirmations. For example, people often say: "It is a nice day," or "I love my kids."

Dzikr is the practice of speaking positive affirmations that originates from Prophet Muhammad. He repeated statements to implant and strengthen his faith. Many of the affirmations used by the Prophet describe God's attributes and how they relate to the Prophet's experience. For example, *Al-hamd-u-lil-lah* ("Praise and thanks be to God") is a *dzikr* affirmation of gratitude.

Throughout history, people have used the power of speech to make reactive statements just to describe (and, thus, reinforce) their unpleasant conditions. Saying, "Isn't it awfully hot today?" is a true statement, but it creates the feeling of helplessness regarding the weather. Making the observation that "Everything is becoming more expensive" creates the feeling that it is difficult for you to afford what you need. But with a little practice, we can make proactive statements about the same situations that create better feelings in us. For example, I can say, "A place of shade feels good in hot weather," and "Everything is becoming more expensive because people have more money and so do I."

The Prophet chose what he spoke consciously to implant inspiring messages within him. He also taught this proactive way of speaking to his companions. This was considered novel, or strange, at the time, and it came to be known by the special name *dzikr*. The Prophet's *dzikr* was mostly to describe to himself the infinite power of God, speaking words of gratitude, asking for guidance and for help again and again. Nothing is impossible if it is the will of God.

Suppose you have experienced events which make you feel like a victim. You feel you are powerless in what has happened, and you are frequently overcome by self-pity. But you realize that to indulge in such feelings is damaging to you. You would like to change the way you feel about the events so you can have a better future.

How do we do it? It often appears impossible to change feelings associated with a deeply hurtful experience into something wholesome. It appears to be an unrealistic idea.

However, experience shows that it is possible for most people to shift their perception gradually by engaging in a process of reevaluating their negative experiences.

In the first step, when you think about how painful your experience has been, you can also wonder why it happened. You can even marvel about it. You can say, "If God is loving, as I believe He is, then I wonder why events took this painful turn? What is the wisdom in what I have experienced? I have heard people say there is a reason for everything that happens. I wonder what positive reasons can be for me to have suffered this loss."

By asking such questions, you shift your mind from being a victim to puzzlement or wonder.

It is possible that initially, you may not figure out answers to such questions. But if you ask this again and again over a period of time, eventually it is inevitable that you will get some answers. "Ask, and you shall be given" is a true statement. You will discover that positive outcomes are possible for you from the difficulty you are going through.

In the second step, you think more about these new possibilities. You dwell on them, and they become more plausible. You can see the advantages that can emerge from what you have gone through. As you see this more and more clearly, you can feel thankful for the new doors that can open for you.

In this way, you shift your feelings from being a victim, to being puzzled, to being grateful. Gratitude is a powerful positive feeling. It attracts abundance to us and opens previously closed doors.

The third step is to realize that the possible benefits you have thought of can actually be achieved. You can go after them. While some of the possibilities feel far-fetched at this moment, it is possible that you will get there with the help of God. As you form new goals, you will meet people who will help you achieve them. Everything is possible with the help of God because God's power is limitless. You now feel confident and energized that great good can come into your life if you take the right action. You become optimistic.

You have now made the transition:
Feeling like a victim—being curious and puzzled—being grateful—feeling strong and optimistic.

These steps are contained in the following practice of the Prophet Muhammad:

When he suffered a setback or experienced something difficult, he said, "*Sub-han-allah,*" which is translated as "Glory be to God." It expresses wonder and puzzlement. Why did this happen when I know that God is compassionate and merciful? There must be some good in it.

Then he said, *"Al-hamd-u-lillah,"* which is translated as "Praise and thanks be to God." He realized that great good can come from what he experienced. He expresses gratitude.

Then he said, *"Allah-u-akbar,"* which is translated as "God is greater than all." Everything is possible with the help of God. The good outcome that has been shown to me is possible. I am going to move forward with it.

This is an emotional scale we can climb:
Anger—helplessness—curiosity—wonder—marvel—gratitude—proactivity—confidence—determination.

Inner healing takes time. The speed of change differs from person to person and the depth of the negative experience you want to overcome. As you persist in changing the feelings inside you, you become better at it, and it proceeds faster with practice. It works even better if you can talk about your efforts with a spiritually aware friend.

I recommend that you undertake such a process of healing for each negative experience that bothers you. The greatest fulfillment in life comes from seeing that your life on the outside begins to thrive as you heal your inner self and to know that you initiated the change, and, thus, feel mastery over life.

19

The Might of God

Sura 13 Ayas 12–13

He it is who shows you lightning; it brings fear in some
and hope in others and raises clouds heavy with rain,
The thunder celebrates His praises and so do the angels
in awe of Him.
And He sends the thunderbolts striking with them whom
He wills,
And yet they argue about God who is mighty and powerful.

Lightning, thunder, and rain are events in nature. They create anxiety and fear in some people, while others experience hope and joy from the same events. The same is true for all our experiences. It is not what happens in our lives, but how we feel about it that affects us. Faith is another name for hope and good expectation, and irrational fear is the opposite of faith. A person mature in faith looks at all things with positive expectation.

All of us have fears. We don't do certain things because we are afraid and our lives are shaped by what we fear. It is, therefore, important to understand our fears.

There are two types of fear. The first is the irrational fear. Some people panic when they hear thunder; some are terrified by the dark; some dread heights; some people are scared of cats, or dogs, or spiders; others fear being alone; the majority of people are afraid of being criticized, or being rejected, or making mistakes.

If you want to grow as a person, you have to become aware of the irrational fears in you and find ways of dissolving them because such fears limit our lives. One way to remove such fears is to think about the fact that these fears are irrational. These are automatic responses in our nervous system for reasons we don't understand. You know from experience that when you felt panic in the past, nothing bad happened. The fear is imaginary and you can train yourself to respond differently. You can write about your irrational fears in your journal and ask how you can overcome them. If you think about it long enough and write about it repeatedly, you can internalize the idea that the fear is false and it will not affect you anymore.

Another type of fear is rational fear. For example, the fear of losing your job in a bad economy, or if you don't do your work properly, or fear that you can lose your health if you regularly overeat. Rational fear can help us because it motivates us to take positive action in enhancing our lives. Fear of God is the fear that if you don't live morally, you are going to suffer. If you break certain rules even if no one is watching, you will be punished because God is always watching. Fear of God is a healthy fear because it prevents us from doing things that harm us.

The thunder celebrates His praises and so do the angels in awe of Him

For those with a superficial view, nature is a set of disconnected objects and events. For those with spiritual insight, the universe is a connected fabric of exquisite beauty, every component of which is an expression of the grandeur of its Creator. The sun, the moon, the clouds, thunder, mountains, winds, spiders, and insects—each has majestic splendor and each sings praises of the Creator in its own way.

There are visible manifestations of nature, such as the mountains, rain, and clouds. But most of the creation is not visible to us. There are forces in the invisible creation which are called the angels. They, too, like their counterparts in the visible existence, are subservient to God and celebrate His glory.

And He sends the thunderbolts striking with them whom He wills

When Prophet Muhammad brought his message of faith to the Arabs, he was opposed by the majority. This can be expected because whenever a radically new paradigm is introduced to a community, there is resistance because of a lack of understanding. Some of his contemporaries even went to extraordinary lengths to abuse and persecute the Prophet. They could not attack him for his character or on the points of his doctrine but were driven by malice, envy, and hatred.

It is reported in Hadith that this aya was revealed to the Prophet after two men came to Medina to confront him. (Their names were Amir Bin Tufail and Arbadeen Bin Rabia.) They insulted the Prophet and threatened to come back with an army to attack him. After they left Medina and were travelling in the desert, a rainstorm occurred and lightning struck Amir and killed him. His friend died soon afterwards from a boil that developed on his face.

In our own time there are people and movements that are working to create better conditions for humanity. While it is reasonable to be skeptical, we should take the trouble of understanding people and their motives before we decide to oppose them. If we oppose, threaten, and work against what is good, we make ourselves vulnerable to loss. It is the intentions within us that determine the consequences for us. If someone makes malice or prejudice or hatred as his primary motive, he can be hit by adversity in unexpected ways, just like being struck by a thunderbolt.

And yet they argue about God who is mighty and powerful.

The power of God is visible in the beauty of His creation and in the laws with which nature works. One of His laws is that human beings shape their lives through their own thoughts. Thus, there is great power and responsibility resting within each of us. If we make good use of it and employ this power to make life better for ourselves and others, then great rewards are in store for us and for those who are with us. If we abuse the power given to us, if we act to harm ourselves and others, if we persistently break the moral code, then pain and suffering come to us in expected and unexpected ways.

20

What Is Good Lasts

Sura 13 Aya 17

He sends down water from the skies, and the streams flow, each according to its measure,

The flood carries away the debris, which comes up to the surface;

Similarly, from the ore, which they heat in the fire to make ornaments or utensils, there is a scum likewise;

Thus does God show forth Truth and Falsehood

For the scum disappears like dross cast out; while that which is good for mankind remains on the earth;

Thus does God set forth parables.

There are many different ideas, philosophies, and fashions presented to us every day. How do we decide what to choose? What is good for us, and what is not? This aya gives an important criterion. What is good for us has been here for a long time. God has preserved it for our benefit. What is unwholesome is temporary; it is washed away by time.

Go to a bookstore and you will see thousands of titles on display. Most of these books will be forgotten in five years. Only a handful will be talked about in twenty years. The really enlightened works will be popular after the lapse of a century. A few books are still alive even after thousands of years.

If you are seeking wisdom, learn from the wisdom of the ages. In addition to the scriptures, these are known as the "classics" in the major languages. There is a reason why Rumi speaks to the hearts of people even though eight hundred years have passed, or we gain flashes of insight from Plato and Plutarch after twenty-five hundred years and we rejoice in the illumination that the verses of Shakespeare bring to us.

This aya validates the value of all scriptures. The Vedas, the Upanishads, the Torah, the Gospels, and all scriptures that have remained alive for thousands of years are here because they contain information of benefit to mankind. The Quran speaks about it explicitly:

He sent down to you the Book with the Truth, confirming what went before it,
And He sent down the Torah and the Gospel before this as guidance for mankind and He sent you the criterion. (3:3–4).

We do a disservice to ourselves if we do not learn from the wisdom and guidance that God has preserved in the scriptures.

Similarly, the classical music of the different world traditions carries themes that have given solace to mankind generation after generation. A piece of music is "classical" because it has been preserved through the ages. It has the divine imprint that connects with the human soul at its depth. It is important to be patient enough to cultivate a taste in classical music so we can experience its value.

Everyone is born and raised in a clamor of feelings, ideas, and prejudices that represent the contemporary culture, and it becomes the template of your own thinking. But among the many ideas you were exposed to, there were statements of spiritual knowledge, the eternal wisdom inherited from previous generations. It is your responsibility to sift through the noise and find what is of lasting value in what you learned as a child. You have then to figure out how to use it. A highly educated but deeply depressed man once told me, "I remember my mother always saying, 'Giving thanks is the door to plenty,' but I never paid attention to what she said because I thought she was naïve."

The art of living is to access wisdom, live and speak it, and bring it to reality in the everyday life of the people around you. In this way, you contribute to raising the level of consciousness that is available to everyone in their daily experience.

The human brain is a powerful machine. It absorbs what you feed it, processes it, magnifies it tremendously, and gives it back to you. If you feed it only the ordinary stuff that makes up most social conversation, your life will become a massive pool of the ordinary. On the other hand, if you take the initiative to regularly expose your mind to texts of wisdom, your life will, in time, become an extraordinary source of inspiration for yourself and others.

Learning of the eternal wisdom requires delaying

gratification. If you go for immediate release of tension and quick shots of pleasure, you will find it in the gossip columns of newspapers. But, if you discipline yourself to learn something of lasting value every day, your effort will be rewarded with a pleasure that will be deep and lasting. An example is a child in school who knows that doing homework is important for his future, but the child cannot resist the easy pleasure of watching television all afternoon. His brother is more disciplined, does his homework first every day, and then watches television. This discipline foreshadows a tremendously more satisfying life for him in comparison with his brother.

The wisdom in a scripture is expressed through the language of the person who first experienced it. As it is transmitted, it is mixed up with the language of the less informed. The meanings and feelings associated with words change from generation to generation. Many people who make an effort to understand the Quran, the Hadith, or other scriptures, are turned off because they "don't understand it." Passages in the book appear far removed from our thinking. Literal readings defy common sense or appear to be contradictory. Many give up and leave understanding of the scripture to the "scholars." This is an unfortunate but common mistake. Unless you do the work yourself to penetrate through the words, you will not know what they tell you.

This experience is similar to learning to appreciate classical music. For the unaccustomed or the one who is used to only the popular tunes, classical music initially carries no appeal. It appears disjointed and unable to hold your attention. But for those who are patient with it and listen to classical pieces again and again, their sublime beauty is gradually and surely revealed. As you persist, you will discover that what makes classical music eternal, or classical books eternal, or classical scenes eternal, are different aspects of the Eternal, which is a name of God.

The insight in this aya is useful in choosing your career. Choose your work such that it benefits mankind and your imprint will be preserved after you are no longer on earth. When you plan your work for tomorrow, or next week, or next year, shape it so it brings benefit to as many people as possible. If you are in a career you feel does not contribute to the greater good, you can begin by deliberately creating the intention within yourself to find meaningful work. Think about this new intention every day and it will become deeper. Eventually, it will attract opportunities from the outside for its fulfillment.

Consider Prophet Muhammad's frequent supplication: *"God, I seek from you knowledge that is beneficial for mankind."*

Finding insights that uplift humanity and teaching it to people was the Prophet's career. He pursued it diligently, and his words have been preserved on earth.

Ideologies, movements, and empires thrive and expand as long as they serve to raise human awareness and well-being. They are removed from the earth soon after their impact on mankind becomes negative. This law pervades all human history. An example from the last century is provided by the rise and fall of communism. When this philosophy first developed, it served to liberate people from the oppression of feudalism, unrestrained industrialism, and corrupt religious institutions. It spread quickly to large sections of the world. As it developed into an empire, it eventually became an instrument of control and oppression; it stifled and enslaved, rather than liberated, and soon after, it disappeared.

Only what is of benefit to mankind is kept on the earth.

21

Tranquility

Sura 13 Aya 28

Those who have faith, their hearts find tranquility in the remembrance of God, for undoubtedly, hearts do find tranquility in the remembrance of God.

No matter who you are, where you live, and what you do, life brings you problems every day. You can be a surgeon, a farmer, an office worker, a business person, a parent, or a student, every day you face challenges. You pursue what you think is good for you. Some of it you achieve, but some of what you want does not work. You experience resistance and opposition, and this creates frustration and disappointment every day. This is the universal human experience.

How you deal with the daily frustrations has a huge impact on your life. If you think of yourself as unfortunate and complain about what is happening to you, the difficulties will multiply and your life can spin out of control.

We need to find ways to dissolve the irritation, frustration, and pain that accumulate daily.

We can obtain relief through the use of chemicals. Tobacco, alcohol, sleeping pills, and other mind-altering drugs make us feel better. The release is temporary, but it works. A big downside is that the substance can be addictive, and it can severely damage your health.

We can also find relief from the pains of life by indulgences, such as eating a lot, sleeping a lot, watching lots of mindless television, or finding fault with what others are doing. These activities also do make us feel better. These also have negative effects on our health and capabilities, and the relief they give lasts only a short time.

This aya points out that you can find peace and tranquility by remembering the presence of God. If you sit quietly for a few minutes and recall to yourself that God cares about you, protects you, and guides you, the turmoil and the fear will disappear, and you experience peace. This practice is called *dzikr,* or remembrance.

It requires faith. As the aya says, *"Those who have faith, their hearts find tranquility in the remembrance of God."* Faith means you are certain that God loves you and cares about you. This means that the difficulties you have are also from God. He created them to improve you, to raise you to a higher level. The problems you are facing feel uncomfortable, but in them, God has hidden the doorways to a better life. My responsibility is to do my best and act with my best intentions. The outcome is up to the beneficent design of God. If you have such faith, remembering the presence of God will create peace and happiness in you.

To acquire faith is a learning process. A person may have been taught the principles of faith, but unless they are internalized, they do not form our spontaneous response to life. We can think we know about faith, but we can still feel that the difficulties we face are because of misfortune. We can complain and blame bad luck or bad people.

There are people who were taught about faith in God as children, but they did not pay attention to it as adults. They did not think about faith anymore. But one day, something terrible happens and they feel fear and panic. They then quickly turn to prayer, remembering God, frantically repeating the phrases they had learned a long time ago. Many find that this sudden turn to faith does not give solace. The words of prayer appear to be remote and meaningless. This is because they have yet to lay the groundwork for faith within themselves.

We increase in faith by consciously internalizing the concept of faith through prayer and remembrance and by interpreting the events in our lives through the concept of faith.

It is a *remembrance*, because each of us has already experienced the love of God in many, many ways, although we may have forgotten about them.

Recall that once you were a little fetus without shape, and it is through the nurture of God that you developed a form as a human being.

You can remember that once you were a little child, without strength or power, and it is by the mercy of God toward you that you have become a functioning adult.

You can bring to mind that there was a stage in life when you were confused and without direction, and it is through the guidance from God that you have found direction.

You can consider that there was time when you were in want, and it is through the bounty of God that you now have means.

You can recall situations in life when you were stuck and you did not know what to do, and something happened unexpectedly by the grace of God and your problem was resolved.

You can acknowledge that you are blessed because you can breathe, you can see, and you can hear. You can remember that you are fortunate you can swallow food and give thanks. You can feel grateful you can walk without limping. Dozens of muscles in your legs and thighs have to work together flawlessly to make it happen by the grace of God.

You can make a list of three things that happened today that pleased you and for which you feel grateful.

Remembering how God has interceded in your life to enhance you is a practice. It deepens our faith, removes anxiety about the future, and creates peace in the heart.

Prayer is remembrance. Consider any of the well-known prayers. When you say them, you recall the benevolence of God for you and for the world. You affirm that God will grant what you ask.

Consider how we remember God in Al-Fateha, the most repeated prayer:

We are grateful to God because He is our Lord, He nurtures us, protects us, takes care of us, and the whole world
He is Compassionate, Loving, Merciful, Gracious
God is the Compassionate Judge, He gives hundreds of rewards for every step we take in the right direction, and He limits the consequences of our mistakes
We serve only You and we ask You for help

The purpose of daily prayer is to consciously repeat this remembrance so the belief that God is our merciful Lord becomes entrenched in our hearts. We have then a strong faith and the vicissitudes of life do not overwhelm us. We can experience peace within ourselves anytime by remembering the presence of God.

For this prescription to work, it is essential that prayer be a conscious remembrance of the favors of God. Mindless repetition of prayer does not increase faith or create peace.

There are people who think that since the Quran is revelation, its language is holy. They believe that repetition of Arabic phrases heals the heart and you don't have to understand them or be conscious of their meaning. This is a false notion.

If your mind is undisciplined, it goes through many diverse thoughts and images continuously. You are thinking of one thing and then your mind jumps to something totally different, then you see an unrelated image in your mind and so on. Since your nervous system, your heart, and all parts of the body respond to what you are thinking, chaos in the mind causes stress and ill health. For people in such conditions, repetition or chanting of any phrase for a few minutes creates a relaxing effect because it arrests the mind's waywardness and produces stillness. You do not require phrases from the Quran for this purpose. Psychologists have discovered that repetition of any phrase, such as "Rose," or "Red," "One," or "Two," can generate the stillness and relaxation.

Conscious remembrance of God as a nurturing presence is a method of personal transformation. As we practice it more and more, faith is internalized in us and

God becomes a reality for us. You feel protected and taken care of. Tranquility and peace replace stress and fear. You believe that everything that happens is good, and you find that it is.

22

Wrong Beliefs Cause Disasters

Sura 13 Aya 31

As for those who are in denial, disasters will not cease to afflict them because of what they do, or will land close to their homes, until God's promise is fulfilled: verily, God never fails to fulfill His promise.

Sura13 Aya 40

Do they not see how We are reducing their land from its outlying border?

A people such as a community or a nation which experiences continuous setbacks are in denial of the truth. They are advised in these ayas to reexamine their beliefs.

Although it is convenient to blame others, the reality is that what happens to us is a consequence of what we do, which flows from our beliefs.

In the country you live in, there are people with different opinions, but there are also beliefs common to the majority of the population. There is a set of agreed-upon principles that appear to be self-evident to the majority. If you spend a few months in another country, you can discover the commonly held beliefs of their culture. Similarly, within a country there are different ethnic and religious communities, each with its own subculture of belief systems, values, and ideals. The level of success and power of each community emanates from their commonly held beliefs.

The results we get are produced by our actions. The actions are consequences of the thoughts we think. But the thoughts spring from our deeply held beliefs. For example, in a country where a common belief is that women are less intelligent than men, women think thoughts of their own limitations and men think thoughts about their superiority over women. This leads to social and political structures that reflect these thoughts. By contrast, in a nation where the common view is that all people are capable of making their own decisions irrespective of gender, the thought patterns are different and so are the social and political arrangements.

What people think about different aspects of life, such as family, ethics, education, government, warfare, etc., is derived from their spiritual beliefs, that is, from what people believe about God and how God's teachings are interpreted and applied. In societies where belief in God is not mentioned in the common doctrine, there are agreed-upon principles about life and its purpose from which laws are derived. For example, in communist countries where the official doctrine rejected the notion of God, everyone was supposed to be loyal to the Communist Manifesto which was believed to contain the complete guidelines for building the perfect society.

It often happens that a community proclaims and teaches its principles and makes efforts to live by them, but the results fall short of the promise. There is failure instead of success; there are disasters instead of triumph. Other communities seem to be faring better than us. What do we do in such a situation? The logical answer to this question is presented in these ayas. If we are getting bad results continuously, it is because we are not acting on the right principles. We should reexamine what we believe. However, this logic has escaped many communities and nations in history.

Many centuries ago in the midst of poverty and chaos of Arabia, Prophet Muhammad received divine revelations. His companions who spent many years in close contact with him imbibed the wisdom and became transformed by it. The passion and the energy in these people was such that Islam quickly spread and became a religion of people in many parts of the world.

However, wisdom cannot be inherited. You can teach the words of wisdom to a new generation, but these are just words. Everyone is born with an ego and grows up with a personality shaped by his or her culture. The work of integrating wisdom into life is an internal process for each person. Many people learn the words, but the words remain outside of them.

In this way, the original positive force of religion dissipates after a few generations. The wisdom taught by Prophet Muhammad is still here in the words he spoke, but we cannot obtain it by reading the words or memorizing them. You have to understand yourself first. We have to learn to be detached from our egos and let go of the many assumptions we have grown up with.

The scenario is very similar with what happened with the teachings of Buddha, Moses, Jesus, and every other religion.

It is easy to learn the letters but the spirit escapes us. Parochialism and nationalism develop around religious beliefs. This prevents people from recognizing that wisdom is universal, that it does not belong to any particular nation or to a particular language. Instead, the community's ego becomes trapped in their rituals and ceremonies. These are often referred to as "our traditions," and there is great pride shown in preserving and defending them. Wars between people of different religions are based on this misunderstanding.

If a community is centered on correct principles, it is flexible in its interpretations of them. There is recognition that although principles of wisdom are permanent, their interpretations change with conditions as time passes. Indeed, flexibility itself is a principle of wisdom. Religious doctrines, philosophies, social, and political theories aim to create a better life. If this purpose is not fulfilled by our interpretation, then it must be revised or discarded. This is an important part of Prophet Muhammad's teaching. He said he did not bring a new religion but simply a reform of what had been taught by the teachers and prophets who came before him. During his own life, he displayed great flexibility. As he and the community of his followers grew and faced changing circumstances, the Prophet's views also changed. New rules of social behavior were introduced on the role of women, economic transactions, war and peace, prayer, fasting, etc., as his community changed over the years. Some ayas from the Quran were abrogated and replaced by others as a part of this evolution.

Fanaticism is the opposite of flexibility. It is the refusal to recognize that if we live with correct principles, we will get good results, and if we experience failure, it is because we either do not know correct principles or we don't understand them. Fanatics are people who think their failure is because of others and not from their own choices. They stick to their beliefs in a blind fashion, unwilling to admit the possibility that change in their own thinking can help them. They are stuck and release their frustrations by hating others.

Persistence is different from fanaticism. Persistence and patience are universally recognized principles of wisdom. In any significant endeavor there is a time lag between effort and fruition; we need to persist in action if we are going to produce the expected result. But a persistent person is also flexible in his approach. He focuses on his own effort and on figuring out how it can be made more effective.

Societies that permit free discussions about their belief systems are much more likely to benefit from the wisdom taught in these ayas. On the other hand, communities that forbid critical discussions become stagnant and are overcome by other more dynamic people.

If we wish to move ahead, it is not wise to focus our energy on being hateful toward those who are oppressing us. It does not help us to speak, again and again, that the enemy is unjust and brutal, usurping our rights without justification. It is not a question of who is oppressing us, but what is making us so weak that others can oppress us. We need to reform our thinking; we need to change ourselves.

We can learn from those who are stronger than us. We should pay attention to how they conduct their affairs. They are stronger because they are manifesting some essential principles better than us.

... until God's promise is fulfilled: verily, God never fails to fulfill His promise.

The universal rules of wisdom are well known. They include sincerity, faith, honesty, compassion, courage, generosity, prayer, proactivity, search for knowledge, etc. It is God's promise that those who will live righteously, that is, live by the right principles, will flourish, and those who do not live by these rules will perish. God does not favor any race or ethnic group. His rules of success and failure apply to all, at all times.

23

Paradise

Sura 13 Aya 35
The parable of the paradise promised to those who are conscious of God is that of a garden,
It is watered by running streams: eternal are its fruits and eternal are its shades,
Such is the destiny of those who are conscious of God—just as the destiny of those who deny the truth is the fire.

This description is a *parable;* it is not a literal portrayal. What does it really say about heaven? Paradise is described in different ways in the Quran, but the images of running water and gardens with fruits and with shade are the most prevalent. To understand the significance of such descriptions, it is useful to know about the climate of Arabia, the region whose inhabitants these ayas were spoken to first.

It is a vast expanse of hot desert. From April to October, the daytime temperature exceeds 100 degrees Fahrenheit in the shade and 130 degrees under the sun. The breeze that touches your face is hot and the sand on which you walk burns your feet. It does not rain for months. Even in winter, it does not rain more than once a month. Vegetation is found in small clumps of trees separated by tens of miles of dry sand. For people living in such a place, finding a stream in which you can cool yourself is the ultimate delight. Similarly, imagine that you walk for several days through the desert and suddenly see an oasis, trees under which you can find relief from the hot sun and you can see fruit on the branches; this is delight. The word for paradise in the Quran is *al-jannah,* "the garden."

All the descriptions of paradise in the Quran: flowing water, dark shade under thick trees, silk clothing, being seated on thrones of honor, fragrant drinks, for a man there are many women who desire him, and for a woman, there is the lasting companionship with her man—these are various ways of invoking bliss and delight.

Please note that bliss, delight, and happiness are *feelings;* they are not material. The objects mentioned are agencies that can induce feelings of pleasure in people. The bliss is not the shade or the silk clothing; it is the *feeling* that you have what you were longing for. You can find this feeling many different ways.

All of us already have experiences of bliss, the times when we were totally happy. The craving of the human soul is to make the experience permanent, to find bliss that does not end. That is what everyone is looking for—to be happy more and more, so that it lasts. To be in a state of permanent bliss is paradise.

You can recreate experiences of bliss. Sit in a quiet place alone. Recall a time when you were completely happy, at peace and you experienced bliss. Now close your eyes and bring to mind the place where you were, see it in your imagination. See who was with you, what you were looking at, what you were saying, and what you were hearing. Recall the smell and the touch you experienced. Pause, take your time and enhance these feelings to capture the original experience. You again are in the same state of happiness and bliss.

Using your imagination to create happiness within you is a form of prayer. Dedicating your life to being in bliss in this manner is the mystic's way of experiencing paradise. A mystic's method is to live on a mountain or in a cloister, sit by yourself and create bliss in your consciousness. Experience shows, however, that this strategy does not work very well if you want to live with people. You have to do things to make a living. You need a home, you have to take care of your children, your body needs care. You have talents you wish to develop, and you desire to make a difference in the lives of others. All such yearnings require you to be out and about.

The Quran gives prescriptions for finding paradise while living a full life. In several suras, it describes traits of people who attain happiness, here and in the hereafter. Consider, for example, Ayas 13:19–22:

Verily, only those with wisdom understand this
Those who fulfill their bond with God and do not break their commitments,
And who keep together what God has bidden to be joined,
And are in awe of their Lord and fear a bad reckoning,
And who patiently persevere out of longing for their Lord's countenance,
And are constant in prayer,

And who give out from the resources We provided for them, privately and publicly,
And who counter evil with good,
It is these that shall enter the house of lasting bliss.

Let us ponder over this advice briefly:

Verily, only those with wisdom understand this

These principles of living are counter-intuitive. Thoughtless people are perplexed by such advice. Only those who can see below the surface can understand.

Those who fulfill their bond with God and do not break their commitments

Your happiness depends on whether people think of you as trustworthy. The only way to achieve this is by always keeping your commitments. Many times it appears convenient or advantageous to not keep a pledge you made. Do not fall into this temptation. Be careful and deliberate about making promises because breaking a pledge to a person is like breaking a pledge to God; it has terrible consequences.

And who keep together what God has bidden to be joined

This has been interpreted by most of the early commentators of the Quran as advice to preserve the bonds of family. Siblings growing together have deep bonds of affection for each other and for their parents. As they grow older, pursue careers and form their own families, personalities and interests diverge. Jealousy comes to the surface as one sibling becomes more successful than the others. There can be competition for prominence and for inheritance. It is easy to break the bonds with your family with the conflicts that adulthood brings. It takes fortitude and faith to keep good relations with your family. When tragedy strikes, when you are desperate for help, when you are seriously ill, when you are old and feeble, most of your friends will not be there. Only people of your family have the instincts to support you and sacrifice for you when you are helpless—if you have worked to keep close to them.

And are in awe of their Lord and fear a bad reckoning

Everything we do has a consequence. Just as living by correct principles leads to a heavenly life, making wrong choices leads to terrible consequences. This is the law of God. We can try to beat the rules of moral living, but we will find that they will beat us every time. A wise person anticipates the consequences of his thoughts and actions and disciplines himself to stay away from what he knows is wrong.

And who patiently persevere out of longing for their Lord's countenance

Making the right choices often entails giving up short-term pleasures. It is taking the uphill road; it often means being shunned by the unwise. A person of faith is patient and sticks to his principles because he knows that the rewards of good action are inevitable; they are guaranteed by God.

And are constant in prayer

The channel between you and God is closed because of the accumulation of debris from years of living without faith. The millions of thoughts of fear, jealousy, ingratitude, anger, and countless actions of unkindness and miserliness have piled up to make a mountain of darkness in your soul. That is why you feel listless when you try to pray. There is no connection. This debris has to be cleared to open the channel between you and God. When you pray once with sincerity and devotion, some of the blockage is chipped away. When you pray again with sincerity, some more of it goes away. If you persist with prayer, you make it a regular and important part of your life, the clearing of debris gains momentum, and then a day comes when you feel a direct connection. Your prayer becomes an experience of bliss.

And who give out from the resources We provided for them, privately and publicly

Know that everything that exists is from God. You are from God, and everything you have is from God. Your talents and your resources are in the same creation in which the poor and the needy are. It is a blunder to become possessive and egotistical about what you have. Spend your resources to make the lives of others better and make the world better. Keep everything you have, your wealth, your skills, your energy, in the flow of God's abundance and the fountain of bliss will find you and take hold in you. Look around and you will find that the happiest people are those who serve others, not those who own the most.

And who counter evil with good

If someone hates you, or is unfair to you, or cheats you, and this induces you to hate and take revenge, you have surrendered control of your being to the other person. You become hateful yourself, and that makes your life hell. Always remember the rule of proactive living: what you do will unfold in *your* life; what the other person does will unfold in *his* life. Each human being makes his or her own future by making personal choices of what to think and how to act. Do not be triggered by the negativity in others to do the same. Instead, create a happy life for yourself by proactively choosing good for yourself and others. If someone hates you, or is unfair to you, or cheats you, and this induces you to have feelings of hate and revenge, but you restrain yourself and do not act on these thoughts, you have demonstrated faith. You can then respond to other person with kindness and convey your good intentions. Great things are in store for a person who learns not to retaliate.

This advice does not imply that you be weak and give in to bullies or bad people. It means, instead, that you have the strength not to absorb the evil from others. This allows you to respond to every situation according to your own purpose, which is to be a source of goodness to the world.

It is these that shall find lasting bliss

Learning to live by noble principles will gradually increase strength in you. As you perfect your character, you will feel an increasing store of personal power. Life will no longer invoke fear, anxiety, and conflict in you. Happiness, peace, and bliss will be your normal state. Once a person achieves a deep sense of happiness, it stays. You do not go back. It is an internal realignment that is not perturbed by external circumstances.

It is a common mistake by lay people and theologians alike to forget that descriptions of heaven and hell are parables. There have been books and essays through history with speculations on the physical nature of paradise, where it could be located, whether it is on the seventh heaven, if it is in our solar system or outside, etc.

A major pitfall of such thinking is that it leads to the belief that you can get there only after you die, that you have to be physically transported there. You are here now, and you have to go to this place out of this world.

This has led many to believe that it is natural to be miserable in this life because happiness is possible only after you leave the earth. This is the mind-set of fatalism. It results in laziness, inaction, poverty, and misery—a life like hell on the earth.

The *parable* of the paradise promised to those who are conscious of God is that of a garden.

24

Gratitude

Sura 14 Aya 7

And your Lord had the proclamation made "If you are grateful I will give you more, but if you are ungrateful, My punishment is severe indeed."

The secret to a life of abundance is taught in this aya, abundance of not only material well-being but also of fulfillment in all areas of life, in loving relationships, in health, in creativity, and abundance of meaningful and productive work. Those who can adjust their thinking to always feel grateful flourish.

If we are grateful, then God gives us more and more. It is a promise. It is one of the ways everyone can experience miracles. You do not have to do anything else. Learn to be thankful and more and more opportunities to give thanks show up in your life.

Gratitude has three parts. One is to speak words of thanks. We notice something good and thank God for it. Thank every person who does you a favor. Prophet

Muhammad said that a person who does not thank people is not grateful to God. The second part of being grateful is to be happy about what you have. All of us have at least a few things such that when we think about them we feel happy and we easily smile. The third aspect of gratitude is to appreciate what we have, to speak well of it, and to take good care of it.

If you find time every day to count the blessings in your life, you will discover that the count becomes longer as more blessings flow into your life. Prophet Muhammad taught people to count on their fingers. To some he said give thanks five times, to others he said ten times, to some others he said count and thank God thirty-three times. He said that after you have prayed, don't rush off but sit for a while and give thanks, counting on your fingers.

There is, however, a major barrier to gratitude. People's attention is quick to go to what makes them unhappy, and they love to complain. The feelings of dissatisfaction can be so strong they rule your mind. Many people are convinced they are more unfortunate than anyone else; they believe nobody has suffered like them. Many live absorbed in hurts from the past. You are here, but your mind is fixated on the unhappiness you suffered yesterday, or a month ago, or twenty years ago.

There is so much to be unhappy about. You don't look as good as you should, your wife is impossible, there are too many other irritating people in your life, you don't have enough money, the weather is always bad, the government is corrupt, and the world is going to hell. It is a miracle you can even function. It has always been like that. You have always felt left out, unable to command your circumstances.

With all the running around you have done, happiness still seems far away. In this state of mind, it is difficult to see anything to be grateful for.

Such feelings of unhappiness are real, based on real experiences, but there is a problem. Unhappiness increases. This is also a divine rule: *if you are ungrateful, My punishment is severe indeed.* The more we complain, the more there is to complain about. If a person believes he or she is unlucky, then that is what life brings to him or her. Your mind notices more and more things to feel bad about. The hole gets bigger the more you dwell in it. We can be so obsessed with what is wrong we are not able to see what is right in our lives.

Prophet Muhammad taught people this prayer:

God, behold, I ask you for a faith that brings joy to my heart with a firm conviction such that I realize that nothing happens to me unless you have prescribed it for me and I feel pleasure at what you have allotted to me, O the most merciful of those who have mercy.

If anyone inculcates this belief, then it becomes true for him or her. The way you are—your body, your mind, your soul, and your personality—are the best possible. Your parents, your childhood, the people you have met, everything that has happened is the best possible. It is the divine plan for you; it has been the preparation for you to live a life of great meaning that God has destined for you. Where you have experienced happiness, it was a great blessing. Where you faced pain and tragedy, it was to strengthen and harden you so you can do great things in life. A person with this belief feels grateful for everything.

He or she is then aligned with the stream of abundance promised in this aya.

Sometimes when a tragedy strikes a person, there is a great shake-up inside and there is a strong urge to vent, to condemn, and to wail. This feels like relief, but the pleasure of relief is short-term. Unless you control your venting, it is going to cause chaos in your life. This is time to be patient, to be humble before God because this is also part of His plan for you. There are solutions to the problems you are facing. A much better life awaits you if you seek it and ask for His help.

All of us run into serious difficulties and painful circumstances. But *God does not burden a soul beyond its capacity* (Sura 2 Aya 286). When a burden falls on me which feels too heavy, it means I am not aware of strengths that are within me which will make this burden light. What I am thinking of as trouble is a reminder that I have much more in me than I give myself credit for. It is an occasion to be happy, to be excited about new possibilities, to ask myself what are the talents and aptitudes in me I am not using that will now come out. I am about to expand, to become more. You can be happy and grateful you have reservoirs of strengths you have yet to discover.

Appreciation for your body is a key aspect for staying healthy. The heart, the eyes, the fingers, the toes, and every other limb and organ in the body is a miracle of creation and gift to us to be used for good purposes. If we are grateful for these enormous gifts, we appreciate our body and take good care of it. We keep it clean, exercise to keep it fit, nourish it with nutritious foods, and protect it from harm.

Some people feel so overcome by the difficulties they

see in their lives they become depressed. They become so disheartened they cannot eat or sleep properly; some are so miserable they have thoughts of suicide. Many seek professional help from a psychotherapist, and many are helped by the treatment. There are different approaches in psychotherapy on how to treat depressed people, but all of them have the same idea at their foundation. You have to teach the patient to think about things in his life that he can be happy about. At first it is not easy, but slowly, he can be coached to notice one or two things that are good. As you become used to thinking of one or two things to appreciate, the space develops in your mind to think of four or five good things. In this way, the focus of the patient's attention can shift to think more and more happy thoughts, to realize that his life is good, that everything that happened in the past was for a good purpose. When a patient comes to believe this, he feels hope for the future and is no longer depressed.

Today, no matter what stage each of is in, all of us can look for things to appreciate and feel happier. We can dig out memories that make us realize how lucky we are. And we can give thanks to open the door for more happiness to flow in: That is all we really need.

25

Words Have Creative Power

Sura 14 Ayas 24–27

Don't you see how God sets forth parables? A good word is like a good tree whose root is firm and its branches reach the heavens.

It gives fruit in all seasons by the will of its Lord.

And God sets forth parables for people that they may be instructed.

And the parable of an ugly word is that of a rotten tree: its root is torn from the earth, it does not have strength to stand.

God establishes in strength those who have faith with words that are firm, in this present life and in the life to come; God will leave in error those who are in the dark; God does what He wills.

The ability to speak is a divine attribute, and it has power. The words a person speaks are connected to images and feelings that represent his or her inner reality. The words are expressions of his or her spirit. They carry energy, and they shape the conditions around him or her. Words, therefore, have creative power.

When you were a baby, you could not speak, but you heard many words. Those words molded your personality. Then you grew up and went to school and learned new words. You listened to friends and to people speaking on television. The words you have heard compose the dictionary of your life. Everything that you believe is possible, or not possible, is contained in the words you have heard.

It is a common observation that some people habitually speak positive language. Their conversation conveys optimism, encouragement, confidence, happiness, and gratitude. What they say gives the impression that life is good and becoming better. Maybe you have come across such people. They seem to lead charismatic lives. Their affairs are harmonious; they attract the right people, and they seem to succeed easily.

There are other people who habitually speak pessimistic words; their talk is about unhappy events, their limitations, disease, doubt in themselves, and envy of others. What they say gives the impression that life is bad and getting worse. They seem to be trapped on the wrong side of life. They often find that their efforts don't pay off, their plans somehow fizzle, and the world appears to be a disappointing place to them.

We reveal our deeply held beliefs in our speech. For example, a person who believes that God is a beneficent force in his life habitually sees goodness in his circumstances. On the other hand, a person whose deep belief is that life is bad habitually expresses this idea in his conversation.

These verses teach us that we can make our lives better by learning to speak better words. The first step is to become aware of the words we routinely speak. With some effort, we can stop using pessimistic and discouraging words to describe ourselves, our children and spouses, our brothers and sisters, our neighbors, our colleagues at work, the people in the government, and people in other countries. We can train ourselves to use optimistic and uplifting words more and more.

Think back and write down one sentence you spoke today that was gloomy or cynical. Then write a sentence that has words conveying optimism and enthusiasm to replace the sentence you spoke. This exercise takes only a few minutes, but when I repeated it every day for a month, it shifted my consciousness to a higher level. I became more aware of what I spoke, eliminated many inferior words from my vocabulary, and replaced them with words of encouragement and hope.

You can change your life by choosing to hear different words. You can avoid company where there is trash talk. You can meet people who have high goals. You can go to hear those who are knowledgeable. If you cannot find such people, you can read books written by them. You can stop going to places where you hear criticism, condemnation, or anger. You can choose to be with people who express kindness, encouragement, and support.

We can make life better by learning new words. The average person uses only a few words again and again. With a little effort, you can increase your vocabulary. People who know more words can express themselves more precisely and more effectively. They can recognize a wider range of feelings within themselves and convey them more accurately. They can understand others better. The leaders in every field know more words and they have learned to use them better.

We speak all the time, and our words are like drops of rain collecting on the ground. They gather into puddles and gradually seep into the ground. They find their way to the roots. Thus, the good words you learn to speak soon penetrate into your subconscious mind where your automatic thoughts and pictures are formed. This, then, creates an autopilot inside you that charts new and higher directions for you and takes you to a better life. It is said in Sura 13 Aya 11, *"God does not change the conditions of people unless they change their inner selves."* You and I can change our *inner selves* by changing the words we hear and speak.

A prayer is a selection of good words. The words of prayer speak of God's compassion for us, His willingness to help us, guide us, and forgive our mistakes. Prayer speaks of our gratitude and our willingness to serve. We benefit from prayer if we are conscious of the uplifting meanings in its words. If someone repeats these words while being aware of them, again and again for months and years, they become embedded in his subconscious and guide him to the life the prayer speaks of.

It is silly to speak good words in prayer and then switch to speaking mindlessly afterwards. It cancels out the benefit you received from prayer. Prophet Muhammad said, *"If you have faith you will only speak of good or keep quiet."*

The human mind is never idle. Conversation goes on inside us all the time, even when we are by ourselves. Anyone who takes control of his or her self-talk gains tremendous power. Instead of your stream of consciousness being random, discipline yourself to speak words to yourself that uplift you. Most people in their self-talk are describing how things are, and in this way, reinforcing their present condition. You can, instead, talk to yourself about how you want your life to be, what you want to see happen. And in due time, you will see it happen.

The practice of choosing your self-talk was called *dzikr* by Prophet Muhammad. Find a book that has words of *dzikr* Prophet Muhammad spoke to himself. Notice what he wishes for himself, how he always invokes the help of God, and how he sets a good intention for everything he does. Model your self-talk after his and your life will soar to heights beyond your fondest dreams.

God establishes in strength those who have faith with words that are firm, in this present life and in the life to come.

The words God uses in the Quran are firm. They are free from doubt, hesitation, and uncertainty. This strengthens and reassures people who believe in these words. When we read the words spoken by Prophet Muhammad, we again notice that his words are always firm and certain, without doubt. We can also learn to speak with firmness so that we create certainty within us, about who we are and what we wish to do.

People with low esteem speak with hesitation. People who have not thought through what they are saying also speak with uncertainty. If we continue to speak in unsure ways, we increase our self-doubt, and this makes us weaker.

We can overcome this weakness by controlling the urge

to give opinions about issues we don't know much about. First, do the work to inform yourself of what you believe in and why. When we speak about ideas we are certain of, we convey assurance and confidence to ourselves and others.

God will leave in error those who are in the dark; God does what He wills.

There are many people who are in the dark about this insight that the words they speak have consequences. There are many who do not believe when they are told that their words shape their lives. There are others who love to talk so much their day is like a spray of words, good and bad mixed together, with little concern about their impact. Those who ignore the wisdom in these ayas use their power of speech in careless chatter that creates more and more chaos for them.

You do not become prosperous if you habitually speak as if you are poor.

You do not raise good children if you often call them bad.

You cannot become healthy if you like to talk about your illnesses.

You cannot have friends if you keep on saying, "I am so lonely."

You cannot become attractive by looking in the mirror every day and asking, "Why am I so ugly?"

You cannot feel good if you repeatedly say, "I don't feel good."

You do not find peace through prayer if you start complaining when the prayer is over.

The power of words is given to people as a divine gift. If you abuse it, God cannot help you because the destructive consequences will be inevitable as result of the power He gave you. Wishing otherwise is not going to help.

26

You Get What You Ask For

Sura 14 Aya 34

And He gives you something out of everything you ask for. And if you wanted to count the favors of God you cannot count them. But surely man is in the dark and is ungrateful.

We can each verify the great truth conveyed in this aya. Everything you have today you had asked for or wished for before you found it. This includes the clothes you are wearing, what you had for lunch, the home you live in, the work you do, the people you live with. God fulfills all or part of what people ask for. You can ask for it by formulating a prayer, or it can be a desire in your mind. It is the same because God knows our thoughts.

To believe that God gives us what we ask for is to acknowledge the might of God and His love for us. Prophet Muhammad said, "*Asking is the essence of worship.*"

You can ask for small things, or you can ask for great things. It is up to you. Prophet Muhammad's advice is,

"When one of you asks for something then let him magnify his wishes, for verily, he is asking his Lord, the most Exalted and High."

What would you like to ask for, knowing that everything is possible with God? The only limitations are those in our own minds.

The world is in need of better ideas, better leadership, better teachers, better products, better literature, and better methods for solving problems. Which of these do you wish to provide? If you have within you the desire to serve one or more of these needs, and you stick with this desire, you will soon learn how to achieve it.

Those who ask for small things get some of them. Those who ask for great things get some of them. For those who make small contributions, there are small rewards. For those who make great contributions, there are great rewards. It is up to each of us if we want to play big or small on the turf of life. God has not placed any limitations for us.

For your dreams and desires to come true, it is essential that you believe they will come true; that is, you believe in the promise in this aya. There will be a time lag between the formulation of your desire and its fruition. You are to be patient in the meantime and strive for your purpose to the best of your ability. Prophet Muhammad said, *"You will be responded to as long as you are not impatient and say, 'I have asked and asked but my request has not been answered.'"*

Consider the second part of the aya: *And if you wanted to count the favors of God you cannot count them.*

As long as a human being is alive, desire is his or her permanent companion. We are always thinking of something we want, something we want to do or to have. When you and I desire something and we think of it again and again, we are shown ideas on how to obtain what we want. We meet people who can help us in finding what we are looking for. This is a great gift God has given to people. Everything we have in our life we found by asking and desiring and so many of our wishes have been fulfilled. If we acknowledge how enormous this gift is, we feel grateful and blessed, and we receive more and more of what we ask for.

Let us consider the last part of the aya: *But surely man is in the dark and is ungrateful.*

Many people are in the dark about the wisdom taught in this aya. They don't realize they can have a better life by asking for it. Instead of wishing and working to make life better, they spend time in complaining about what they have, and as a result, remain stuck there.

Many people feel they are trapped by their circumstances. They have the belief that the obstacles in front of them are insurmountable. We hear people say, I want to do many things, but I can't because

- I am poor
- I am not educated
- I am too old
- I am a woman
- I live in a small town
- I am too dark
- I am married to the wrong person
- I am too busy
- I have allergies
- fate has dealt me a bad hand

Such beliefs reveal a misunderstanding about God. A person who thinks likes this has the view that God does not have the power to melt the obstacles in his or her life. Prophet Muhammad said, *"Supplication can overcome fate."*

What makes us unhappy has great value because it makes us think of possible alternatives. Because of the pain we feel, we can imagine what a better life would look like. We can then ask for it and plan for it. We can feel joy in the knowledge that God hears us and responds to our requests. We can believe that God gives us everything we ask for except those things that are not good for us. If we persist with faith, in due time, we see our circumstances change to produce what we have been looking for.

27

Divine Spirit

Sura 15 Ayas 28–33

Behold! Your Lord said to the angels: I am about to create the human being from clay and mud molding it into shape.

When I have fashioned him and breathed My spirit into him, bow down prostrating to him.

So all the angels bowed except Iblis; he refused to be with those who prostrated.

"O Iblis," said God, "why is it you are not with those who prostrated?"

He said, "I am not going to bow before the human being whom you made by molding clay and mud into shape."

This allegorical description of the origin of the human being contains several important truths. One is that God has infused His spirit in mankind. That is why nothing is impossible for a human being. The spirit in us has the resourcefulness to make life into what we want. We have to switch our focus away from thinking of ourselves merely as bodies toward remembering that the divine spirit lives in each of us.

There is much mystery about what the spirit is. But we know that the body is visible and the spirit is invisible. We access the spirit through the invisible parts of our personalities, through what we are feeling and thinking. These aspects of us are very powerful because they are expressions of the spirit. The course a person's life takes is determined by what he or she thinks and feels.

Because the spirit is from God, it is eternal, although the body in which it resides is temporary and it perishes. The thoughts we think, the feelings we feel, and the words we say are realities forever. You can easily recall how you felt twenty or thirty years ago. And the experiences that have receded from your memory are still recorded in your subconscious.

The body is precious because it is the housing for the spirit during its journey on the earth. It is important to keep our bodies healthy so that the spirit is not distracted from its mission of healing the world by becoming absorbed in repairing its living quarters. However, it is an inversion of priorities if you spend more effort in taking care of your body than you devote to the cultivation of your spirit. Also, if you are unhappy for a long time, your spirit becomes distressed and it will show up as physical symptoms in your body.

There are ninety-nine divine names. These are attributes of the spirit. God is the perfection of these attributes. We human beings also possess the same attributes to a lesser extent. Our spiritual journey is to elevate and perfect the divine attributes in us.

Being loving is a divine attribute, and this attribute is

also found in humans. God's love is unselfish. He does not love anyone because He gains something from giving love. He loves you for your sake. He expresses love by creating conditions in which you can be more aware and make better choices for yourself.

When we human beings love someone, there is often self-interest mixed in it. The more we become aware of this and learn to be unselfish and love the other person for his or her sake, the closer we get to manifesting divine love. When we do something to raise the awareness of another person, we are expressing divine love. Most people come close to this experience when parenting a small child. They love the child for its own sake without having any expectations in return. Also, when we do a favor for a stranger whom we don't expect to see again, we are expressing divine love.

For a person who knows about love and its healing power, it is possible for them to love everyone. God loves everyone, and we can also love everyone who comes into our lives. We may not like a person, but we can still have love for them. We can think well of them. We can pray for them. We can do things to help them become more aware of the choices they are making.

Being angry is also an attribute of God. Thus, it is said in Al-Fateha, *"keep us away from the path of those who have earned Your anger."* God's anger is for the sake of the person with whom He is angry. God is egoless, and He is not angry because His feelings were hurt or He would lose something by what you did. The purpose of God's anger is to help human beings become more conscious. If you are on the wrong track, He first creates troublesome events to serve as reminders. If we don't pay heed to those, then more painful consequences follow. In reality, God's anger is a part of His love for His creatures. It is reported in the book of Bukhari that Prophet Muhammad said, "*When God created the creation He pledged to Himself by writing in His Book, 'My love always prevails over my anger.'*"

An example of the manifestation of this quality in humans is when a parent gets angry with a child to warn him or her from doing something that would hurt the child. However, when we get angry because our feelings are bruised or we are tired or simply because we want the other person to obey us, then we are acting from the ego, and this type of anger hurts us.

God is spirit and "*verily His command is such that when He intends something He says to it: Be, and it becomes*" (36:82). Human beings share in this power of the spirit but to a lesser extent. Human speech also has creative power. If you think about it, you will realize that most of what is happening in your life at this time is from what you have intended and spoken in the past. If you want to change your life, you can do it by making different intentions and by speaking differently.

The spirit is so powerful that people can create intentions within themselves and achieve them. This gift is in humans from the beginning. Have you seen a toddler move across a room? He looks at where he wants to go and starts moving. If he falls on the way, he gets up and keeps moving until he gets to his desired destination. It is the same mechanism for adult people. If you set up a goal for yourself, keep your focus on it and keep going, you *will* get there. Adults have problems in benefitting from this wisdom because they have a tendency to look to the right and to the left instead of where their goal is. Notice that the toddler does not look here or there. She looks at only where she wants to go. She does not spend time worrying about how bad it is that she fell on the way.

"O Iblis," said God, "why is it you are not with those who prostrated?"
He said, "I am not going to bow before the human being whom you made by molding clay and mud into shape."

Iblis does not recognize the power in man because he looks only at the physical—"clay and mud fashioned into shape." Iblis forgot about the divine spirit in the human being and is therefore the symbol of the wrong way of thinking, the one who misguides. Whenever we look at people only in terms of their physical appearance, we are also misguided. That is why categorizing people by race is evil.

When people think of each other only as bodies and have sex, it can give physical pleasure in the short-term but creates dejection and disgust in the long-term. On the other hand, when people know each other deeply and are united in their spirits by love, then their sexual union is bliss that lasts.

People are aware of their physical senses, and it is easy to recognize the body and its needs. The spirit is invisible. Becoming aware of it occurs through indirect ways. The purpose of worship is to make us aware of the spirit. For example, the word for prayer is *salat* which means to connect (with the spirit). Similarly about fasting it is said, "*Fasting is prescribed for you as it was prescribed for those who came before you, so you can grow in awareness*" (2:183). Some people become aware of the spirit through music. Others have extrasensory experiences that make them aware that they are more than their bodies.

It is said in Sura 2 Aya 156, *"surely, we are from God and we are surely on our way returning to Him."* This describes the journey of life for everyone. Each of us becomes more aware of the spirit as time passes, some more and some less.

28

Hope and Faith

Sura 15 Aya 56

And who but those who have gone astray abandon hope of the Lord's mercy?

All of us can find ourselves in situations where we face daunting obstacles. You or someone you love can be severely ill, your business or career can be in a crisis, or you can be badly hurt by people you love. There are people who have been wrongfully arrested and put in prison for long periods of time. There are women who have been abandoned by their husbands and left with children to raise. You feel like you have fallen into a well and there is no way to climb out.

What do you do in this situation? How do you view such a situation? It is logical to feel hopeless. All the discouraging evidence is there. The doctor has shown you the scans and where the tumor is. You cannot deny that the trouble you are facing is real.

But there is an alternative, if you have faith. You can

say to yourself: What I am seeing with my eyes is really a small part of the whole picture. The complete state of affairs is known to God. He is most compassionate and merciful. His grace is always present. He created me, loves me, and is in charge of my affairs. I trust Him completely. I am sure there will be a positive outcome from the situation I am in. I have placed my trust and hope in God.

Hope and fear are attitudes *within* you, and you have a choice in adopting either of them. Your life will evolve differently based upon your choice.

There is an important difference between attitudes of despair and hope. In both, you are making pictures in your mind about the future. You are in the here and now, but you are forecasting the future in your mind.

If you are experiencing fear and doom, you are making pictures of unhappiness in your mind. You are expressing a belief that you are helpless, your life is terrible, and worse things are about to come.

If you make a different choice and discipline your mind to experience hopeful thoughts, you are making a different forecast about the future. You are saying, I am not alone, God is with me, and He has infinite power. God will turn things in a way that is best for me.

Depending on what forecast you are making in your mind, you will experience different emotions, your imagination will create different scenes, and you will take different actions. What we decide to do emerges from the pictures we have in our minds. Fearful and despairing people act differently than people who have faith and hope. They also attract different kinds of people around them. People without faith try a few things, and if success does not come quickly, they give up. People with faith have hope. They don't give up. They keep trying different ways until they succeed.

Today, people are concerned with three areas of life: relationships, health, and finances. There seems to be a consensus that you need to succeed in these areas in order to be happy. With the knowledge and the resources available today, there is no reason why everyone cannot find happiness in these important areas of life.

Some people are unhappy in their marriage relationship; some have issues with other close family, like parents or siblings or children. They experience continuous friction. Others are unhappy because they are not married. Life is lonely, and you cannot find someone good and wholesome interested in marrying you. This unhappiness can become the all-consuming emotion.

For many others, there are problems related to health and the body. For some, it is the presence of serious illnesses. For others, it is how they look. For quite a few people, the major struggle is with the condition of their bodies.

For many people, it is the lack of money. This is often related to the struggle to succeed in their careers. They feel they deserve to do better financially, they make plans and work hard, but somehow, it does not work out. You will find people for whom this frustration is what consumes their thinking.

There is another kind of concern which drives quite a few people among Muslims. It is the unhappiness about the state of the *ummah*, the oppression experienced by many Muslim people and the powerlessness of Muslims in controlling their situations. This is a source of great unhappiness for many people.

In all situations where we see apparently insurmountable obstacles, this aya gives us this advice:

And who but those who have gone astray abandon hope of the Lord's mercy?

Does this mean that faith in God is enough and we are not to do anything? The answer to this is clearly no. We change our circumstances by taking action, by doing things. However, what we do and how well we do it originates from the state of mind we are in. The Quran often speaks of "Those who have faith and do good works ..." You will notice that in all such ayas faith is mentioned first and then action. First, we have to do the internal work of centering ourselves in positive belief. You have to convince yourself that the Lord *is* merciful toward *you*. We are then guided to the right course of action, and our actions are fruitful.

If you are unhappily married, your relationship can be healed or you can find a better partner. If you are alone, you can find someone who loves you. Your relationships with your parents, children, and siblings can be loving. If you are sick, you can recover and be healthy. If you think you are ugly, you can become good-looking. If you are poor, you can be well off. If you are stuck in your career, you can find work that is rewarding and fulfilling.

We are human beings. We have the ability to change what we are thinking. We can erase fearful pictures from our minds, and we can stop ourselves from talking in discouraging ways. Instead, we can speak faith in our self-talk and in conversations with others. We can do this in all circumstances, even when our situation appears to be bleak.

We can leave the company of those who are discouraging and fearful. We can find the company of people who are cheerful and encouraging.

When worry strikes, you recognize that it is negative thinking and it harms you. Switch your thoughts into a prayer. Think of what you want and ask for it. Prophet Muhammad said that to ask for what you want is the essence of worship.

In Sura 65 Ayas 2–3 it is said:

And for everyone who is conscious of God, He grants a way out of unhappiness, and He provides for him/her in ways beyond all expectation, and for everyone who places their trust in God, He is sufficient.

Al-Fateha is the most repeated prayer. You may recall its last aya which says:

Keep us away from the path of those who have earned your anger and who have gone astray.

Those who have gone astray is a translation of *ad-dualleen*, which is precisely the same word used in Aya 15:56 for people who give up hope. It says those who give up hope in their affairs have gone astray. You and I know how to come back to the right path. We can kindle hope in our hearts. We can hope for our Lord's mercy and a better life will surely unfold.

29

Take Care of Your Team

Sura 15 Aya 88

Don't look with envy at the good things We have granted to some others, and neither be sad over them, but spread the wings of your tenderness over those who have faith in you.

In any long-term endeavor you are engaged in, whether it is to raise a family, establish a business, start a religious community, or change the world by social or political action, you are working with companions who share your vision. But you can become discouraged by looking at others who are more successful than you. This aya advises us not to look wistfully at what others have. Instead, we should focus our efforts on nurturing those who are with us.

There is very little that a person, however talented he or she may be, can accomplish alone. There are many brilliant ideas in books written by ingenious individuals which went nowhere because there was no team to implement them. Therefore, a crucial component of carrying out any plan is to build and maintain a team of people who care about each other and their purpose. Having companions who share your purpose results in miraculous progress because the power of the human spirit multiplies tremendously in supportive company. One plus one is really more than eleven.

For example, when people get married, they are acting on the wisdom that you are much more likely to find happiness as a team than by yourself. The marriage is successful only to the extent that you can maintain trust and love. You have to learn to cooperate with each other toward common goals of raising and educating children, helping each other be physically and emotionally healthy, making your home a pleasant and safe environment, and building financial well-being. A marriage flourishes more if it is supported by people in the extended family who are committed to the couple's happiness.

A business is a team with the purpose of making or selling a product. The business can succeed if it has a team of people who work together with positive attitudes toward each other and who believe in the value of the product.

Many organizations are formed with the purpose of doing social good or bringing about political change. Only those succeed where there is a team that has mutual trust and long-term commitment to their ideals.

A mosque, a church, or a temple consists of a group of people who seek guidance from a particular scripture. There is spiritual growth in the community if they can worship together in a spirit of harmony and devise goals on which they can work together.

There is a lag time in creating significant new results. This is how nature works. If we want to grow food, we have to till the soil, remove weeds, fertilize the ground, plant seeds, deal with bad weather, and wait for our efforts to bear fruit. Similarly, in any significant human endeavor, there is a period of waiting between the formulation of our plans and their achievement. The mission has to go through a lean period in which you put in the effort and there is no visible fruit. If you are committed, you have to learn to deal positively with frustration during the waiting period.

In the meantime, we can see others who are more successful than us. They are in the limelight and not us. This can be very discouraging. God advises the Prophet in this aya not to look longingly at what others have and not be upset because they don't pay attention to his message. Instead, concentrate your efforts on what is crucial to your success, and that is to nurture those who share your vision.

Love and harmony are the essential ingredients from which the power of a team is derived. Two people may have different personalities and different cultural backgrounds, but they can like each other for the sake of the goals they share. But if the personal differences become more important than the common purpose or there is rivalry, the team loses its power. Sometimes even one person with a quarrelsome or distrustful personality is enough to derail a large group.

The metaphor used in this aya is that of a bird that lowers its wing in loving solitude over its young. Your task is to nurture the people who are with you by caring for them, by supporting them, by being concerned about them, by strengthening them, by loving them. The basic glue that holds any group together and gives it power is love, and we must actively seek to love one another if we want our team to accomplish its mission.

Since "love" is a word with which people associate different meanings, it is important to clarify the spiritual meaning of love that is conveyed in this aya. The Prophet is being asked to love the people who have faith in his mission. Spiritual love is more, much more, than a feeling. It is seeking to promote growth in the people you love, to expand their capacities, to help them overcome their limitations.

Perhaps the meaning will become clearer if we also describe what love is not. Love is not dependency. If the people you love are not able to function independently of you, then they will not have the confidence to do things to help themselves or contribute to the purpose of the team.

Love is not obedience. In order for you to grow to your potential, you have to become your own person; you need the freedom to develop your own thinking. You can contribute to your own life and to the common mission only if you are free from the feeling that you have to obey another person.

Many well meaning people seeking spiritual guidance become trapped in groups where "love" is taught as obedience and dependency. There is a guru or a sheikh who is assumed to know the Truth, and the price he demands for teaching it is complete obedience. The sheikh decides when you wake up and go to sleep, when and how you pray, and when and whom you marry. Such misguided arrangements are destructive to the spiritual growth of all concerned.

The spiritual love mentioned in this aya is enabling and non possessive. The bird who spreads her wings on the young wants them to fly, and if they hesitate, the mother bird pushes them out of the nest, forcing them to spread their own wings.

30

Certainty in Faith

Sura 15 Aya 99
And worship your Lord until you find certainty.

Belief that the All-Mighty God is your Lord and Sustainer is the most fundamental of all religious teachings. God is all-powerful and God cares for us, provides for us, protects us, and guides us. It is the most fundamental belief because it can be the most empowering belief, if you have it.

Although large numbers of people do believe in God because of the teaching they received in childhood, very few consciously deepen it to turn it into the powerful foundation of life it is meant to be. For most people, belief in God becomes mixed up in their experiences of guilt and pain of their growing years.

All beliefs are self-fulfilling. It is, therefore, in my own interest to form the belief within myself that God cares for me, provides for me, protects me, and guides me. If I believe this to be true, then it is natural for me to think that every good thing is possible for me. It means the pain I have suffered is because God is preparing me for a better future, and I do not have to be afraid at any time, because God is my protector.

In the Book of Muslim a Hadith Qudsi, attributed to Abu Huraiyrah, is reported in which Prophet Muhammad said: *God, all glory and praise is to Him, has said, "whatever My servant assumes of Me, that is how I am to him, and I am with him as he remembers Me."*

If I deeply believe that God is loving and merciful, it will be true for me. If I believe that God is not here, but lives in the heavens, then that will be true for me. If I believe that God is always with me and protects me then it will be true for me.

The real spiritual challenge is not to prove the existence of God but to correct and deepen your belief about God. I need to install the belief in me that God, the All-Mighty, is my Lord and Sustainer. He cares for me, provides all my needs, He cherishes me, protects me, and guides me.

The obstacle in this quest is the discouraging and half-hearted beliefs we already have about God. The work involved is to remove the limiting beliefs and replace them with empowering beliefs about your relationship with God.

We should be aware that belief has depth. You can state your belief in words such as: "God is compassionate and loving." You can say it and not really mean it; maybe you have never thought about what it means. For some, it can be a deeply held belief, or it can be somewhere in between. Half-hearted prayer is useless. What we believe *deeply* shapes our lives.

Belief is strengthened in two different ways:

The first way is to recall events from your experience

that demonstrate that the belief is true. Think often of the ways in which blessings have come to you and it will create the conviction in you that God loves you and cares for you. Dwell on the miraculous way in which you were nurtured when you were in your mother's womb, and after you were born, the amazing ways in which your heart, your eyes, your hands, and other parts of your body work in harmony. So many people have cared for you and loved you. Teachers have brought you knowledge. So many of your desires have already been fulfilled, some without any effort on your part. Also choose to look at and appreciate the gifts in your surroundings, the comforts in your home, the majesty of the landscape, the sun, the moon and the vegetation, the bright of the day and the dark of the night, and you will gradually become aware of the loving presence of God with you. This is the path of worship through gratitude.

Belief is also deepened by conscious repetition of statements of faith. The words we speak shape our awareness, and words we speak again and again become deeply instilled in us. This is the path of worship through affirmations.

Thus, repeatedly saying, "God is most compassionate and merciful" instills this idea in the person who says it.

Being conscious means you are aware of what you say, you have thought through the words you speak in prayer. A person who repeats affirmations consciously gradually experiences the feelings that the words convey.

Most people cannot relate to traditional words of prayer. It is more effective to render prayer in your own words, words you understand and feel.

Repetition of words with positive feelings establishes

positive beliefs in us. Conscious prayer also overwrites previously held limiting beliefs. Persistent repetition creates the positive beliefs at deeper and deeper levels, removes doubts, and creates certainty. Hence, we are told in this verse: *worship your Lord until you find certainty.*

God gave Prophet Muhammad the mission to teach people to believe in the true invisible God and abandon beliefs in false deities. He diligently worked on the mission, but for many years, only a few people were convinced of his message. The majority rejected him and some ridiculed him. It is in this context that God says to him:

We do indeed know how your heart is distressed by what they say
But celebrate the praises of your Lord and be of those who bow in prayer
And worship your Lord until you find certainty (15:97–99).

Please note that in the first two ayas God advises the Prophet to switch his focus from a negative thought to a positive thought. He says, "I know you are upset, but don't be sad about your lack of progress. Instead, think of the goodness you have received, *celebrate* it, and give praise and thanks. That is going to help you." Second, be steadfast in your worship such that you become certain that the All-Mighty God is your Lord, your sustainer, your friend, and protector.

This was the advice God gave to the Prophet. Each of us has circumstances in our lives in which we are facing frustration. Some people have difficulties in their families, some are worried about their finances, some are trying to move forward in their careers, and some are concerned about reforming society and find that no one listens to them. The advice given in these verses speaks to all of us. Stop yourself when you have thoughts of frustration or failure. Shift your attention to what you can be happy about, celebrate the gifts God has bestowed on you, and give thanks. Create a deep belief in the benevolence of God, engage in prayer to create certainty in yourself, and the might of God will come to your aid.

31

There Are Resources Everywhere

Sura 16 Ayas 10–18

It is He who sends water from the skies; from it you drink and so do the plants which your cattle eat.

With it He causes crops to grow and olives and dates and grapes and all the fruits. Surely, in this there is a message for people who think.

And He has made the night and the day and the sun and the moon subservient to you; and the stars are subservient by His command. Surely, in this, there are messages for people who use their reason.

And what He created on the earth has many shades of colors. Surely, in this, there is a message for people who reflect.

And He it is who has made the sea subservient, so that you can eat fresh meat from it, and take from it ornaments you wear.

And on the sea you see ships going through the waves, so that you may seek to enrich yourself of His abundance, and thus may be grateful.

And He has placed firm mountains on earth, lest it sway with you, and rivers and roads, so that you can find your way, as well as many landmarks: and by the stars people find their way.
Is, then, he who creates like one that cannot create? Do you not consider this?
For, should you attempt to count God's favors, you could never exhaust them.

We human beings live in nature. From early childhood, we observe, experience, and react to plants, animals, oceans, rivers, clouds, the breeze, the sun, and the moon. How we relate to nature and interpret its forces is, therefore, of interest to everyone. This topic is discussed by scientists, philosophers, and common folk alike.

There are several viewpoints about nature:

One view is that nature is vast, big, and it works by its own rules impervious to human existence. The winds blow back and forth, the oceans swell and recede, the stars move in their circles, the sun and moon shine and go into hiding, all according to forces acting on them. The human species live on a small planet that is like a speck of dust in the vast galaxies that surround it. What possible significance can be there for a species in a condition of fleeting existence on a tiny planet? There is good evidence to substantiate this view.

Another view of nature is expressed by admiring its beauty. The moonlit night, the warmth of the sun on a beach, green meadows with flowers, the cool breeze on a hot day, these images create pleasant feelings. This view is often invoked by artists and poets. And there is merit in this perspective.

Still another popular view is that the physical world is a source of danger and hardship for us. The oceans create storms that flood towns, causing death of many people, destroying houses and property. The changes in the sun create extremes of hot and cold that cause suffering and death. Also, the rains are never constant. Sometimes, we have too much rain, causing destruction by flooding. At other times, we have too little rain, resulting in droughts which cause starvation and death. There is a lot of evidence to support belief that nature is destructive.

Nature as a source of fear is the basis of religion in early human history. People believed that extraordinary power resides in the sun, the moon, the winds, the rain, the sea, and in animals. People worshipped them and offered sacrifices to them so they would be safe from the wrath of natural forces. Some people believe that the sun and the moon aligned in certain conjunctions with the planets bring bad luck and calamity.

Please note that these ayas present a different view of nature. They say that objects in nature: the rain, the sun, the moon, the stars, etc., are a source of benefit to mankind. Moreover, God says He has made these forces subservient to us. They can be tamed, and we can derive benefits from them if we use the faculties we have.

The other interpretations of nature given above are based on physical evidence. The Quran's point of view is based on an important spiritual reality, which is that the human being's perspective is creative; the reality we experience is made by how we think, and we have the ability to choose what and how we think.

Thus, if a group of people live in fear of nature, the fear can make them superstitious, and this can limit their life possibilities. If, on the other hand, you believe that everything you encounter has benefits in it for you, then you are going to look for them and likely to find them. People's lives are made by the perspective they adopt. If we realize that the nature around us has resources that sustain us, enrich us, and guide us, then we can live with an attitude of appreciation and gratitude. Such a positive outlook brings us in harmony with creation and allows more and more goodness to flow to us.

For, should you attempt to count God's favors, you could never exhaust them!

Only a few objects have been mentioned in these ayas. If we understand the principle, we will know that everything we experience has benefits for us. The material and spiritual benevolence that surrounds us is unlimited. This is another way of saying that God is Beneficent, and we can invoke this belief with conviction in everything we do by saying: *With the Name of God, the Beneficent and the Merciful.*

In one sense, everyone's life is different and human beings experience a great variety of circumstances. But in another sense, all human experience has this fact in common: On any day, you can encounter objects and events that can cause fear, anger, or frustration. But we have the option of disciplining our thinking and shedding such negative feelings. Instead, we can ask these questions: What benefit could be there in this situation? What can I do so I will come out stronger from this situation? If you ask such questions, you will find answers sooner or later. Acting on these insights, you can derive benefits from the situations that at first appear to be painful or unpleasant.

On any given day we also have experiences that bring happiness, joy, and satisfaction. It is important that we pause and acknowledge them. If none seem to occur, we can feel pleasure by appreciating the beauty of moonlight, the warmth of sunlight, the colors in a flower, or the innocent look of a child. The best way to make our lives better is by looking at things around us that give us happiness, to experience feelings of being blessed. This opens the door for more blessings from the limitless store of goodness God has created.

Qualities That Unlock Abundance:

Notice that these ayas point to several human qualities that should be used to recognize the deeper meaning of existence. I have copied the ayas again below and printed the qualities God asks us to use in italics.

It is He who sends water from the skies; from it, you drink and so do the plants which your cattle eat.

With it He causes crops to grow and olives and dates and grapes and all the fruits. Surely, in this there is a message for *people who think*.

And He has made the night and the day and the sun and the moon subservient to you; and the stars are subservient by His command. Surely, in this, there are messages for *people who use their reason*.

And what He created on the earth has many shades of colors. Surely, in this, there is a message for *people who reflect*.

And He it is who has made the sea subservient, so that you can eat fresh meat from it and take from it ornaments

which you wear.
And on the sea you see ships going through the waves,
so that you may *seek to enrich yourself* of His abundance, and, thus, *may be grateful*.

And He has placed firm mountains on earth, lest it sway with you, and rivers and roads, so that you can find your way, as well as many landmarks: and by the stars people find their way.

Is, then, he who creates like one that cannot create? *Do you not consider this?*

For, should you attempt to count God's favors, you could never exhaust them!

Thinking, using your reason, reflection, consideration, seeking to enrich yourself , being grateful are the special human traits that allow us to see behind the superficial and grasp deeper reality. It is inspirations from ayas like these that guided the early Muslims to explore nature and become leaders in science and technology.

Use of these attributes allows human beings to overcome fear and relate to nature in a rational manner. With thinking and intellect, people have found immense resources hidden in nature that can be turned to advantage to make life on earth a heavenly experience. Consider these examples:

We have found that water can be turned into electricity, this way, you can have light at night time.

Plant fibers can be made into cotton.

Worms yield silk.

Mold makes penicillin that cures infections.

The pull of gravity can be used to fly airplanes.

The precise orbits of the sun, moon, and the stars can

be used to guide vehicles to other planets.

Soil has an abundance of silicon which you can use to store huge amounts of information to make computers, telephones, and many other devices.

With application of technology, farmers can grow more and more food from smaller and smaller plots of land.

There are countless examples like this that you are already familiar with.

Is then, he who creates like one that cannot create? Do you not consider this?

In different branches of science, people have learned to reflect, think, and reason in ways that unlock the great benefits that are hidden in nature. Great varieties of inventions in physics, chemistry, biology, and engineering have opened the doors for better and better life for all people. Economists, historians, and artists also use their minds in creative ways to make life better. Such creative people are the pride of mankind. By asking a rhetorical question, this aya encourages each of us to use our creative faculties and contribute to human progress.

In our present culture, the majority of people do not think of themselves as creative. There is a popular and false notion that artists, writers, and scientists are somehow different from everyone else. In reality, the creative force is in all of us, and it is expressed by using the faculties mentioned in these ayas: thinking, reflecting, and reasoning. You have to stop thinking of your life as a grind and find ways to put across your creativity.

32

Those Who Do Good Find Good

Sura 16 Aya 30

And when it is said to those who are conscious of God,
"What is it that your Lord has revealed?" They say,
"What is good."
For those who do good there is good in this world, but the
reward in the hereafter is better still; for how excellent
is the abode of the God-conscious!

Religion and its impact on humanity have two sides. Religion is acknowledged as a source of good, wisdom, and morality. The majority of people believe in religion and is convinced that their redemption is through the beliefs they hold. They find inspiration in the scriptures. On the other hand, the history of the world is replete with oppression, cruelty, and other types of evil carried out in the name of religion. People have interpreted scriptures, the revealed Word, to justify abuse of women and children, discrimination against minorities, slavery, economic exploitation, and genocide. In addition, many people who think they are religious oppose science and hold beliefs that are manifestly false and attribute their attitude to revelations. Many make rules of unhappy living, creating misery in their homes in the belief that they are obeying the Word of God.

With the backdrop of this common human weakness, this aya points out that those who are conscious of God find the goodness that is in revelation. Those who are conscious know that He is benevolent, and His messages are from His grace and mercy. The purpose of revelation is described at the beginning of the Quran in Sura 2 Aya 4. It is to guide mankind to *falaah,* i.e., success, happiness, peace, and prosperity. It is to help us find all that is good.

The second part of the aya says there is a simple formula for finding goodness. Do good and good will come to you here and in the hereafter. It is not very complicated or philosophical. Train yourself to overcome the bad tendencies in yourself. Live conscientiously. Take the initiative of being a source of goodness and you will achieve a happy state. This is worth emphasizing because this central idea escapes most people. They have come to believe that religion is a complex set of rules and arguments which only scholars can understand.

People get confused by revelation because its language is often transcendental. A literal or superficial reading results in meanings that are misleading. It takes contemplation and patience to discern the guidance in revelation. There was a context within which events described in the scripture occurred. We want to be aware of the historical and social context before we extrapolate their meanings to the present.

Our emotional histories color our views. The images

and sounds that are reverberating through our minds filter what we understand from a text. We have to learn to be quiet inside in order to open our hearts to revelation.

Some people are misled by revelations because they are invested in the status quo. The current system gives them advantages over others, and they interpret religion to justify the present order.

Some deduce inferior meanings because they derive national or tribal pride from "our religion." They discuss the scripture to find meanings that helps them look down on others, or oppress others, or make war on others.

People who are conscious of God search for the best meanings; those that give insight into wisdom and liberate people from limitations. This aya tells us that people who manifest goodness are the ones who are conscious of God. Do not be misled by special robes or elaborate rituals or other pretenses. Those who have risen above their egos and have become conscious are those who have goodness in their own lives and create goodness for others.

If you misunderstand revelation, you can infer meanings which make you unhappy. You may think you are following the rules of religious life, but you can be miserable and stuck. Many people justify failure in life by saying to themselves, "I may be unhappy now, but I will find the rewards of my prayers in the next world!" This aya contradicts this notion. It says if you do good, you will find good in *this* world. The hereafter is a continuation of the present. So if your life is not working, reexamine your beliefs and change your interpretations.

The second part of this aya teaches the basic law that what we send out into the world comes back to us. So if you want to change your life for the better, then get busy doing good, and inevitably, your life will also be filled with goodness. The word "good" includes everything that makes you or others better; it includes positive thought, speech, and action. It means thinking well of yourself and others; it means speaking well of yourself and others; it includes creating a positive intention within your mind when you do something. It means dropping negative thoughts and speech; it means not to look down on what God has given you in your person, or your experience; it means letting go of anger, jealousy, hopelessness, and self-pity; it means never wishing to harm anyone. This is what we do when we become God-conscious, because we know that what we are thinking is known to God, and He compensates us for everything we think, say, and do.

For those who do good, there is good in this world, but there can be a delay, and it can work in indirect ways. You may be kind and generous toward someone, and he can respond with hostility. This type of experience occurs commonly and throws off a lot of people. They say, "I was being good, but it was not returned to me. This formula of goodness for goodness does not work. It is better to hold back and see what others do first. If they act good toward me, then I can take a chance." This is a misunderstanding. The good that you did is a reality; it is guaranteed to bear fruit. It will come to you later, perhaps through other people. Prophet Muhammad said that the greater the delay, the greater is the reward for you.

Many people become confused about revelations because they borrow the meanings from someone else. They say, I am not learned in religion so let me find an expert. If you try to live through someone else's mind-set, your life becomes complicated and difficult. The other person did not have the experiences you did. If you wish to understand something and use it, you have to figure it out yourself. You can use wisdom only to the extent you personalize it.

There is another difficulty when we look to others to find meanings. There are many people who can give impressive speeches about things they don't understand. They can talk about it, but don't know how to do it. There are many who have written books about subjects they don't understand. There are people who can dress up to look like authority figures. The only thing that a person really knows is what he or she is able to do. It is the walk you walk and not the talk you talk that matters.

Prophet Muhammad was neither a scholar nor did he study to have a degree from a religious academy. He learned to be conscious of God through his own search, and he understood the spiritual truths in simple ways that he could apply to raise awareness in himself and in others. He teaches us to do the same.

33

What Do You Believe?

Sura 16 Aya 35

Those who ascribe divinity to other than God say: "Had God so willed we would not have served anything other than Him—neither we nor our forefathers; nor would we have forbidden anything without His sanction."

Thus also said those who went before them. Yet what is the mission of messengers except to communicate clearly.

This aya addresses four questions that deeply impact everyone's life:

1. What do you think about God?
2. How do you relate to what you have been taught by the previous generation?
3. How do you decide what you can or cannot do; i.e., what prohibitions are important?
4. What is the role of a teacher?

Let us discuss these one by one.

1. People have believed in God for thousands of years but often in ways that have limited them. Many think of God as someone who controls human beings. This aya cites people who use this argument not to believe in God. They say, if God is in charge of everything, why does He not make us believe in Him? This type of argument is still used by people who consider themselves atheists. It is based on the mistaken notion that God is someone who lives in heaven above and pulls the strings of everyone living on earth. They often argue that if God exists, why do we have wars or earthquakes, and why do many children die young. Such a point of view is a misunderstanding of what God is, and of the relationship between God and man. The reality is that human beings have the freedom to choose their beliefs, and their lives evolve according to what they believe.

Let us ponder over the implications of this freedom. We think continuously. This is human nature. We cannot ever stop the pictures, ideas, and feelings that are flowing through our minds. The ideas we think of again and again crystallize into beliefs; i.e., repetition causes us to believe in some ideas to be true. What we believe determines what questions we ask and what actions we take. In this way, the thoughts we think continuously shape the life we lead.

For example, if you want your life to be better but you see many problems around you and you think that you are too weak compared to the obstacles you face, it can be difficult for you to take much action. If, on the other hand, you believe that God will help you in your efforts, then it can be easier for you to take action.

It is important to pay attention to the image of God in your mind and to improve it. The famed psychoanalyst

Carl Jung said that no other belief has a greater impact on a person's life than his or her view of who God is. Everyone has heard about God and His attributes from parents and teachers, and these remain as hazy notions. Your spiritual power begins to gather when you focus on improving your personal view of God.

Recall the Hadith Qudsi in which God says, "*whatever My servant assumes of Me, that is how I am to him, and I am with him as he remembers Me.*" This tells us that God has given us the freedom to choose our relationship with Him. If you believe there is no God, then He is not there for you. If you believe that God takes care of you, then He does.

I recommend that you read a well researched biography of Prophet Muhammad to see how he acted on this concept in his life.

He believed that God was always with him and guided him.

He believed that God helped him in everything he did.

He believed that God had given him his life's mission and supported him in achieving it.

He believed that God sent angels to fight on his behalf in battles against his enemies.

He believed that his prayer was a direct communication with God, and that God responded to his prayers in ways which was best for him.

He believed God helped him in all his personal affairs also. For example, when he had water to drink, he said, "I thank God for making this water so sweet." When he came out of the toilet, he said, "Thanks be to God for healing my body and removing the unwanted from me," and so on.

The books of Hadith describe how the Prophet

interpreted every event in his life, big or small, happy or painful, as help from the Almighty God.

What Prophet Muhammad believed about God became true for him, as it does for each one of us. How would your life change if you develop beliefs similar to his about your relationship with God?

2. *The second part of Aya 16:35 says: "nor would we have prescribed prohibitions other than His."*

There are prohibitions, or taboos, in every society, and also in families which become internalized in the lives of individuals. Where do they come from? Many are based on superstitions, cultural traditions, or historical accidents, and limit the possibilities in life. Over the years, I have lived with different groups of people who believed in the following prohibitions:

- Don't start a new venture on a Friday if it is the 13th of the month.
- Don't marry someone whose astrological sign does not match yours.
- Don't marry someone who is not your own kind.
- Widows should not marry.
- Women should not go out of the house.
- Women should not go to the mosque.
- A woman cannot lead prayer.
- A man without a beard cannot lead prayer.
- A woman cannot teach from the Quran.
- Music is forbidden.
- Smiling is forbidden.
- Makeup is forbidden.
- Toothpaste is forbidden.
- Never speak of a good thing that happens to you

because it can bring bad luck.

- No one can be gay.

And people believe in many other such rules. Many taboos are based on irrational fear. Some of the social prohibitions are prejudices designed to keep the disadvantaged in their place. Many rules of prohibition are couched in religious terminology to create an aura of authority. This aya asks us to question the taboos prevalent in our surroundings. Where did they come from? What is the wisdom in what people think to be taboo?

Obviously, there are things we should not do because they would harm us, or those we love, or the world as a whole. We absorb most such rules of behavior from family, friends, and other influences in our surroundings. A conscious person evaluates his rules and discards those that are against his conscience or are contradicted by evidence.

3. *So said also those who went before them.*

If we let superstitions and prejudices of our ancestors dictate to us, we ascribe authority to other than God who wants us to live consciously and take responsibility for our lives. Human civilization is evolving, and it is the responsibility of each of us to contribute to its progress. We have to work to enhance the goodness we have inherited from previous generations and filter out ideas and customs which limit opportunity and freedom.

4. *But what is the mission of messengers except to communicate clearly?*

A teacher can explain principles of wisdom to us, but the responsibility of the teacher stops there. It is up to us to do the work to understand words of wisdom and change them into plans of action. It often happens that we hear something we think is insightful and can help us, but we forget it in a few days. The new idea bounces off from our habitual stream of thinking.

On the other hand, if you are a teacher, this aya points out that your role is only to explain to the best of your ability. It is not to control or judge people who do not respond in the way you think they should. Everyone has within them the capacity to make their own decisions.

34

Uplift Those Below You

Sura 16 Aya 71

God has bestowed more resources on some of you than on others: yet they who are more abundantly favored are often unwilling to share their gifts with those who are under their authority so that they might be equal in this respect. What! Will they, then, deny that these favors are from God?

There are many opportunities for getting ahead in life; but not everyone is able to make use of them equally. This is because everyone is different. Some are born in better circumstances, some are physically stronger than others, some are more intelligent, some are more resilient, and some have the capacity to work harder than others. It is inevitable that some rise higher than others. This aya asks those who have gained authority over others to recognize it as a favor and to use it to uplift others.

An important theme here is that the qualities we have are bestowed on us by God. It is opposite to the ego statement, "I did it all by myself." Let us think of some of the things that give a person power and how he or she gained them.

Maybe you were born in a well-to-do family. Obviously, your will had nothing to do with it. Your good fortune is a gift you received from God.

Maybe you became smart by the learning you received in a school or college. Knowledge that has been gathered by humanity over thousands of years was condensed in books you read. It was taught to you by teachers who have spent their lives learning this material. These are important gifts that contributed to your success.

You learned useful business skills because someone taught them to you. If you had ideas to succeed, you were motivated by someone. Your ability to make good decisions came about because you were exposed to an environment where it was possible.

Perhaps you rose to a position of authority because someone gave you a break. They thought well of you and gave you your first job or a special opportunity.

Your good looks and physical strength have contributed to your success. You did not choose them; they are from the genes you inherited as a gift from God. Your looks and your strength will disappear unless they are supported every day by nutrition in the food you eat. Hundreds of people you don't even know contribute to growing, transporting, and cooking the food you consume. It is a great gift without which you cannot even survive.

All the beneficial influences that have uplifted you and me have been given to us from a complex network that spans great distances and many generations. These are manifestations of God's bounty. This aya asks us to recognize the river of benevolence that has raised us and give back. Become a part of the stream to raise those who are less than you in status and achievement.

Trust and motivation are the main forces that determine the success of an organization. A business where managers are jealous about guarding their advantage is built on distrust. The workers have low morale, and there is low productivity. In a business where the managers work actively to uplift and nurture their subordinates, there is greater loyalty to the organization and greater productivity. The same dynamic works in any organization, whether a family, a school, a social club, or a political party. If the higher-ups in the hierarchy are generous in nurturing those under their authority, the organization flourishes.

In order to share our expertise with our subordinates, we need faith. We have to overcome the anxiety that if we uplift someone, then he or she can become strong and challenge our authority. This may very well happen. There are people who take advantage of a benefactor and double-cross him or her. Such a response can cause us discomfort in the short-term. But we can be sure that in the grand scheme of your life, every act of giving will produce tremendous rewards. It is a mistake to be inhibited from doing good by fear that the other person will not respond in kind.

35

Make Yourself Strong and Resourceful

Sura 16 Ayas 75–76

God gives an example—someone enslaved, owned by another, has no power over anything, and someone else whom We have given good resources from ourselves and who spends from it at will, both privately and publicly. Are these two equal? Praise and thanks be to God: but most of them do not understand it.

And God gives the example of two men—one of them dumb, powerless, and a burden on his master: to whichever task is he directed he brings no good.
Can such a one be considered the equal of someone who commands justice and is on a firm path?

In both of these ayas, two categories of people are described. In the first aya, there is a comparison of someone who is unable to act on his will; he or she is described as enslaved, versus someone who is resourceful, free to act, and is generous in helping others.

In the second aya, the comparison is between a person who is powerless and clueless, unable to do anything right, versus someone who has the strength and the authority to guide others and to pursue his purpose.

In both ayas there is a rhetorical question: can these two people be considered equal in their ability to do good? The answer is obviously no. God wishes you and me to be resourceful and have the ability to accomplish our objectives and help others.

The idea expressed in these ayas is an important evolution of religious thought. Before Prophet Muhammad, many people had presented religion and spirituality as "unworldly." Seekers on the path of God often lived on charity. People were considered close to God if they lived in caves, on mountain tops, or in cloisters, devoting their lives to worship. Among the ordinary people who did not take such extreme measures, those disengaged from life's challenges were considered more godly and spiritual.

Notwithstanding these and other similar statements in the Quran, this misunderstanding is commonplace even now in the Muslim world. Many people believe that someone who is weak, prays a lot, and does not do much else is religious. Many professional people think they will turn to religion after they retire because what religion teaches is useful only for the next world. You meet many people in mosques who appear to be helpless, confused, and incapable of doing much.

One major difficulty in learning about religion is that there are so many interpretations. First, there is the interpretation you learned as a child. Then if you want to advance your understanding and listen to scholars, everybody has a different view. How do we decide what the right interpretation is?

These ayas give us a criterion. Any belief, any tradition, any interpretation that does not make you more resourceful, more powerful, and freer to act is false. Stated in the opposite way, the right interpretation is the one that if you act upon it, it will increase your personal power to make a difference in your life and that of others.

If religious teachings contribute to personal growth, resourcefulness, freedom, and happiness of people who follow them, then these represent the true purpose of religion. If, on the other hand, religion is taught in ways that contribute to constriction of human potential, to unhappiness and lack of productivity, they are false, regardless of how famous the scholar who conveys these ideas.

For these reasons, we can see that all the interpretations that women should be subjugated, or their movements be restricted, or their choices should be controlled by men, are misguided interpretations. Any religious opinion that tries to limit the rights or opportunities of any group of people is a false interpretation.

With the same distinction in mind, there are two different ways in which Aya 75 can be interpreted:

"God gives an example—someone enslaved, owned by another, has no power over anything, and *someone else whom We have given good resources from ourselves* and who spends from it at will, both privately and publicly."

One point of view is that of predestination, that God has made some people poor and others rich, and He made some people weak and some powerful; we have no choice but to accept how things are. This interpretation leads to fatalism, resignation, and weakness.

The other view is that within each person God has

placed His own spirit, so there is great potential in every human being. Those who cultivate the talents given to them become resourceful, and those who neglect their talents become weak. God has not only given talents and intelligence to the human being, but also the initiative to apply them. We should, therefore, strive to develop what has been given to us and become resourceful. This interpretation leads to proactivity and empowerment.

You know about the life of Prophet Muhammad. He was an orphan in Arabia, a place where there was no civilization: no schools, no libraries, no roads, no agriculture, not even a history of past accomplishments. The people were tribal and continuously fought each other. He discovered faith through which he empowered himself and those around him. He generated personal, political, financial, intellectual, and moral power for himself and others, where there was none before. You can, thus, see that his interpretations of religion were those that created strength and resourcefulness. The crisis in the Muslim world is that degradation in interpretation has occurred over time.

Let us consider the practice of prayer. It was the foundation of the Prophet's practice and teaching. By all accounts, prayer was the main source of his strength. His prayer was in his own words, and expressed his heartfelt feelings. It was his conversation with God. He said you can change your destiny through prayer.

But for many people now, prayer is a ritual of words and movements that mean little to them. Many pray under a feeling of compulsion, with their minds filled with doubts and distractions. This makes them feel confused and weak. In order to benefit from prayer, we have to understand the principle of prayer. We should find time every day to be deeply quiet so we can feel the proximity of God. Discover hope, optimism, and connectedness that exist in words of prayer and feel these feelings in your prayer. The power of prayer is in what you are feeling inside. Discipline yourself to pray with feeling several times a day, and your life will soar.

Let us consider the traits of successful people mentioned in these ayas:

whom We have given good resources from ourselves and who spends from it at will, both privately and publicly

A successful person spends from his or her resources. At every point in life, you have some resources at your disposal. This includes your money, your time, your physical strength, your ability to think and speak, your freedom to love and bless people. In order to be successful, you must spend from these resources; that is, put them into use for a positive purpose. There is a saying that if you don't use something, you will lose it, and the opposite of this is also true: our resources multiply when we put them into action to uplift our own lives and those of others.

In Aya 76, the successful person is described as:

someone who commands justice and is on a firm path

You can have many goals, but the overarching goal of an enlightened person is to make the world a fairer place. The human consciousness is in a process of evolution. Our past is animal-like, with thinking focused on possessiveness, self-centeredness, competition for survival, and prejudice against our competitors. Our future is one of abundance, harmony, inclusiveness, equality, and peace. The role God has assigned to each of us is to contribute to this process of positive change. We fulfill our purpose when we spend our resources to make the world a more just environment. Work to remove prejudice, exploitation, exclusivity, and distrust, and instead, bring advantage to those whom history has made disadvantaged.

Do not dwell negatively on aspects of your life where you are weak and do not beg for justice. Instead, think of where you are strong and *command* justice; i.e., make it happen with your power. No matter what your life situation is, you have relationships in which you have influence. Most people have this authority at least in the home. Make sure that you deal with your children in a fair way, and not discriminate in favor of one against the other, and similarly, be fair in your relationship with your spouse, your siblings, and in-laws. Make sure to be fair to people you buy from or sell to. Look into your thoughts and remove prejudices against ethnic or religious groups. If you work to create fairness in your immediate life, your influence will increase, and you will gain the authority to contribute to a greater part of the world.

36

God Has Blessed Us in So Many Ways

Sura 16 Ayas 78–81

And God has brought you out from your mothers' bodies not knowing anything—but He has given you hearing and sight and feelings, so that you may be grateful.

Have they not seen the birds flying in the air? None but God holds them up. In this surely there are messages for people who have faith.

And God has given you houses as places of rest, and tents from skins of animals—easy for you to handle when you travel and you camp—and furnishings and goods for temporary use from their skins and their wool and their hair.

And God has made for you, in what He created, means of protection: thus, He has given you places of shade in the hills, and garments to protect you from heat and cold, as well as such garments that protect you from danger.

In this way He bestows blessings on you, so that you might acknowledge Him.

Let us begin with the first aya in this sequence:

And God has brought you out from your mothers' bodies not knowing anything—but He has given you hearing and sight and feelings, so that you may be grateful.

Our senses and our feelings are the resources with which human beings create their lives and the world around them. This aya is asking us to recognize how immense this gift is. The human baby is weak, vulnerable, and without information, but it has these faculties. It has been gifted with the ability to see, to hear, and smell, to learn, to remember, to relate to others, and to think. These are the faculties with which we accumulate knowledge, gain power, and create our circumstances. Do not undervalue these gifts because everyone has them. And there is no limit to how much you can learn, what you can think, and what you accomplish. All human achievements, big and small, are accomplished by the application of these gifts. Where you start out and your physical size are not the relevant factors, but your human attributes are, because these are divine gifts with miraculous powers. If you recognize their true value, you will be enormously grateful.

This leads to the next aya which has deep meaning:

Have they not seen the birds flying in the air? None but God holds them up. In this surely there are messages for people who have faith.

How do you think God supports the birds flying in the air? Perhaps He has many hands, one for each bird!! The Arab contemporaries of Prophet Muhammad thought of

God as a being, like a super-creature or like a man, and they made images and idols to represent God in many ways. Even today, many think of God as a person living in the sky. You have to bring sacrifices and offerings to keep Him happy. This aya points to a very different way of thinking.

The Quran says that God cannot be described or made pictures of because He transcends all creation. Anytime you try to describe God in human terms, you will be on the wrong track. God has created people, and the same God has created laws that govern the physical world. They include the laws that govern how the air moves and how a bird or an airplane can fly in it.

In this surely there are messages for people who have faith. Think about how birds can fly, think about the nature of the world and how it works, think of the possibilities that are outside of your experience. If you have faith, you can learn new things and expand out of your present perceived limitations, just as you have already gone beyond what you could do as a baby. Use your faculties; they have the power to take you beyond your present condition. God has created an orderly and beneficial universe with infinite possibilities. The laws of God are working in all parts of the universe. The more you investigate them, the more you can learn about them, and the more you can grow.

A spiritual law related to this discussion is stated in Aya 14–7:

And your Lord had the proclamation made "If you are grateful I will give you more, but if you are ungrateful, My punishment is severe indeed"

To see its relevance, let us look again at Ayas 80–81:

And God has given you houses as places of rest, and tents from skins of animals—easy for you to handle when you travel and you camp—and furnishings and goods for temporary use from their skins and their wool and their hair.

And God has made for you, in what He created, means of protection: thus, He has given you places of shade in the hills, and garments to protect you from heat and cold, as well as such garments that protect you from danger.

In this way He bestows blessings on you, so that you might acknowledge Him.

These ayas mention a miscellaneous list of objects, houses, and tents, wool and clothing, places of shade in the hills, etc., that God has created for us. It is saying, take time out to think of the many objects around you that support you and comfort you. Acknowledge these gifts from God and you will experience great increase and expansion in your life. Do not make the mistake of ignoring the good in your life.

In a state of lack of faith, people have the tendency to ignore what is helping them and obsess with what is bothering them. This is a trap in which people can get stuck, and it is like a hole that gets deeper and deeper. The more we focus on what we are unhappy about, the more we attract unhappy events in our life. Another way of saying this is that God punishes us if we live with an attitude of ingratitude.

We can escape from this trap by doing what these ayas are teaching us. Be sure to acknowledge the many gifts you have in your life. Even if we are facing great problems, there are *some* things we can think of which are helping us and for which we can feel grateful, such as: I have a room or a home where I can rest, I have clothes that protect me from hot and cold, I have the ability to hear and to speak, etc. Changing our focus from what is not working for us to what is helping us, however small it appears to be, shifts your spiritual energy from negative to positive and brings it in alignment with God's law of abundance. Think hard and look at all layers of your life and acknowledge everything that supports you, helps you, and comforts you.

Everyone who has reached great spiritual heights developed ritual practices for doing so by focusing their attention on the good in life. This is because they know the rule: "If you are grateful I will give you more."

Here are two examples from the habits of Prophet Muhammad:

Ali reported that when Prophet Muhammad donned a new piece of clothing, he used to say this: "I praise and thank God for this garment which adorns me before people. It covers me and it adds beauty to my life."

Ibn-Umar reported that he heard the Prophet speak thus before going to sleep at night:

"I praise and I thank God Who provided for me sufficiently today, gave me shelter, and gave me good food and drink.

He enhanced me and favored me in everything I did, and bestowed His gifts on me generously.

I thank God, and I praise God as I am.

He is the Lord of all that exists and the Owner and Master of all that exists. I seek His protection from taking the wrong path."

It is a powerful way to conclude each day on a positive note, and it can make a major difference in how well you sleep and what your mind thinks the next day. Practicing gratitude proactively on a regular basis will keep you in touch with the very best of your possibilities. It will enable you to see opportunities and utilize resources which may otherwise have remained hidden.

Does this teaching mean that we should ignore our problems and never talk about them? The answer is clearly no. In order to move higher in life, we need to recognize the problems that come our way and make plans to overcome them. It is the mind-set with which we consider our problems that makes the crucial difference. Talking about problems obsessively or continuously, perceiving ourselves as victims and expressing hopelessness prevents us from seeing the opportunities for betterment that are always nearby. Noticing the goodness that is present under all circumstances and giving thanks for it is a method of rising above our problems.

In these ayas, Bedouins living in the Arabian desert fourteen centuries ago are being told they can build many things from the resources they have: places of rest in the hills, the wool and the skins of animals, etc., because they have been gifted with the ultimate resource: sight, hearing, their minds, and hearts.

What about us today? Have you met people who think they cannot do anything in life because they have no resources, they had bad breaks, they are too young or too old to do what they want to do, they are over qualified or under qualified, or their parents did not treat them well?

These ayas show how to get out of this boxed-in attitude. First, we can remind ourselves of the fact that opportunities in the world around us are infinitely more abundant today than in the past. Moreover, the most powerful resources that human beings have are within us: our basic God-given faculties. It is how we choose to apply them that makes the difference.

37

Be Fair and Generous

Sura 16 Aya 90

Behold, God enjoins justice and the doing of good, and generosity towards people and He forbids all that is shameful and that runs counter to reason, as well as envy; and He exhorts you repeatedly so that you might bear all this in mind.

Here is an important series of dos and don'ts in this very famous aya; it is commonly recited at the conclusion of the Friday sermon.

The first advice is for us to be just and fair in dealings with others, and not to be swayed by prejudice or selfishness in making decisions.

"Doing of good" is a translation of the Arabic word *ehsan*. It is derived from *husn,* which also means beauty and grace. God is asking us to deal with others graciously and with goodness.

We are all familiar with the concept of generosity. It means to help others with what we have; not to withhold help from others because of fear that you would become poor.

Then the aya reminds us of three negative traits we should discard. They are as follows:

The first is not to act shamefully. All of us have within us a set of rules of goodness and morality. We call these our conscience. Anything we do that is against our conscience creates shame and self-criticism in us. It is shameful because it lowers your own view of yourself. If you persist in behavior that you believe to be shameful, it will sooner or later bring shame to you.

The aya asks us not to do things that are counter to reason. Life continuously offers us opportunities to make choices among conflicting options. It is easy to make decisions based on our weaknesses, such as fear, envy, greed, or prejudice. There are people around us who convey various types of superstition, cynicism, and negative thinking. The advice in this aya is to use your head in making decisions. Gather facts and act morally and rationally.

Next, there is a warning against being envious. It is common for people to feel envious of those who are more successful than they are. People commonly express their envy by bad-mouthing those they are envious of. It is a self-defeating emotion because it focuses your mind on your lack of success. It is very important, for your own sake, to discard such feelings. Instead, make a habit of praising the good fortune of others. This shifts your thoughts to good things that are possible, your thoughts are positive, and they attract abundance in your own life.

There is a political interpretation of this aya which is popular. It suggests that those in power have the ability to be just and generous, and, therefore, this aya is describing how government officials should behave. They should be fair and take care of people in a generous way. The government should banish things which are hurting the people. This view motivates people to political action.

There is also a personal application of this aya. It says that each of us has a domain in which we are the "government," where we have control. It can be your home or your place of work. For every human being, there is also the domain of his or her mind. Exercise the attributes of fairness, generosity, and doing good in the kingdom that is in your control. Banish thoughts of envy from your mind and other thoughts you are not proud of. Who do you think will benefit if you decide to have the best possible thoughts in your mind from now on?

To convince yourself that this aya is a method of self-empowerment, you can compare two families that you personally know. Consider the family where people make an effort to be fair toward each other, are generous in helping each other, and take the initiative in doing good. Such a family will be happy and prosperous. By contrast, if you have a family in which people act unfairly toward each other, they are unable to evaluate each other's actions in a generous way, where there is jealousy between the parents or among the siblings, the life of such a family is chaotic and dysfunctional.

You can also compare communities. A community is prosperous if the people are fair, where people know that if wrong is done to them then they will be fairly compensated, where people are generous toward each other and toward others, and take the initiative of doing good to each other. There is admiration and support for those who accomplish something instead of envy or leg-pulling.

If you think about these traits only superficially, you can say that they are all very good and you then move on with your familiar patterns of life. If, on the other hand, you think about them deeply, you will be convinced that internalizing these traits and making them a part of your person is a spiritual path that will transform your life to one of fulfillment, power, and contribution. But this requires personal change. You need to know about the deeper patterns within you that prevent you from acting on the ideals described in this aya.

There are subconscious patterns within each of us that dominate our thinking and our behavior, and most often, are not visible to us. The task of spiritual growth is to unmask these patterns and to replace them with thoughts and behaviors that you choose. This is accomplished through contemplation, self-evaluation, and finding the company of like-minded others who are also on a similar path.

The Quran describes ninety-nine divine attributes. Justice, generosity, and doing of good are among them. As a human being integrates these traits within himself and is able to manifest them in his life, he succeeds in his role of being God's agent on the earth. God blesses such a person and showers abundance and rewards on him.

38

Make a Lasting Contribution

Sura 16 Aya 96

What is with you passes away, whereas that which is with God is enduring. And We shall give to those who patiently persevere their reward according to the best they did.

Human beings have a special gift: deep down in their souls, everyone believes they want to make a lasting contribution; they want to make a difference in the world. This is the voice of the Divine Spirit in mankind. There is another side to the human being: the self-centeredness, the desire for quick gratification. This is the ego side of him.

For the majority, the life of the lower-self has become normal. The idealism and the dreams of doing good have receded. They are caught up in a daily routine focused on their own wants.

This aya is reminding us of this distinction. You can live a great life, a life of lasting significance, by changing your focus from the humdrum and the trivial to the lasting values espoused by God.

How do you decide what to do? What are the criteria you use to prioritize items on your "to-do list" for the day, for the week, and for the next year?

Everyone's list reflects a hierarchy of values.

1. There are things we do to meet our body's needs, to survive and to be comfortable. Examples are eating and sleeping, cleanliness, taking steps to be healthy, relaxing, having a pleasant home.
2. There are things we can do to meet our ego needs, the urge to show off, to prove you are better than others. You can compete more fiercely for small things, gossip to put others down, act out of jealousy, buy a bigger house or car or more expensive clothes so you can feel superior to others.
3. There are things we can do to contribute to the lives of others by providing them comfort, good counsel, or material help—people in your family, friends, and strangers; the people you impact through your work.
4. You can be invested in a large purpose of enduring value and work systematically toward achieving it. Examples are helping build a school or hospital, help an organization that works to uplift people's lives, remove poverty, ignorance, cruelty, injustice, prejudice.

How enduring the impact of a person's life is depends upon how they choose to mix these four criteria on a daily basis.

The Quran teaches us to make item numbers three and four our major focus. That is where the lasting value is, and it is here that divine attributes can be revealed in you. On the other hand, what we do to please ourselves through items one and two will not take us anywhere; it is of fleeting value. Surely item one is important for survival, so do take care of your needs, but don't live there; instead, live your life as God's agent, to change the world for the better. What you do for the sake of God is everlasting; what you do for yourself is temporary.

What positive effect will the success you desire have on the world around you? If your vision of success is all about you, its fruits will disappear with you. But when you expand your vision beyond yourself, its impact will last beyond you. Rather than being in it just for yourself, look for ways to create real value for others. That is how you create lasting success.

Humanity is in a state of spiritual evolution. This is reflected in the struggle inside every person. Every human being has within him the tendency to be self-centered and also the desire to be a source of goodness. And everyone chooses the balance between these two urges depending on his or her spiritual state. This aya is teaching us to be aware of this and strive to go higher. It really depends on how much you value your life. Do you want to just live a fleeting life and be extinguished like a moth? If you do not leave a trace in the world, what is the difference whether you live for eighty years or eighty minutes?

If you examine your life in the light of the four criteria listed above, you can see for yourself where you are on the spiritual staircase, and which way you are moving. When a person becomes conscious of the mix of values they are living by, they also get the ability to move up to higher values.

There are relatively few people who choose to live

according to item number four. These are the people who decide on a purpose bigger than themselves, and they live to fulfill that purpose. These are the people who shape the world and whose impact lasts for a long time.

We are at this time living in the culture of consumerism. It uses sophisticated advertising to convince us that a wonderful life is to be busy spending your time and resources on consuming ever-increasing varieties of products. This drowns the lives of many people in the ever-deepening swirl of self-indulgence.

To create a life of lasting value requires being different from the herd; it requires having your own mind; it requires marshalling your time and resources for your purpose.

If you wish to make a major difference, you need faith and patience.

Faith, or *iman,* means you believe that God gave you life for His purpose. Your life is not going to be in vain. God's help comes to those who strive to live a life of benevolence for the world.

Sabr, or perseverance, is the other quality needed by anyone who wants to make a difference. When you think of changing something for the better, you quickly see many difficulties in your path. Only if you understand the value of being patient and persevere in your efforts, even if there is no visible progress, you have the possibility of reaching your goals. Prophet Muhammad said that patience is an essential part of faith.

Patience enables you to overcome anger, frustration, confusion, and anxiety. Patience is more than just waiting. Patience is having the faith and the confidence to act over the long-term, beginning now, and steadily continuing day after day until your goal is reached. Large achievements require time. When you have the patience to continue making the effort, you will achieve your purpose.

Think of anyone who has made a major difference. Like anyone else, they made mistakes as they learned and grew. But because of the great good they did, they are remembered by the best of what they did. God reminds us in this aya that this is a rule that applies to everyone. God invites us to live by the lasting values so He can reward us also with the measure of our best contributions.

39

Faith Rekindles Your Life

Sura 16 Aya 97

As for anyone, be it man or woman, who does what is good, and has faith—We shall certainly revivify, and give him or her a fulfilling life; and We shall give them their rewards according to the best they did.

For many people, life has become a dead end. They look to the future with despair. This comes about because of wrong values, having selfish and manipulative attitudes. The Quran refers to people in such a state as if they were dead.

Benjamin Franklin observed that most people are dead when they are twenty-five but are buried at sixty-five. While humanity has much improved since the time he spoke these words, it is still true that many people feel permanently unhappy and don't see a way out. They cannot do what they want to do. Some do not know what they want to do with their life. Some live to please others and feel miserable because of it. Many are depressed. It seems there is no choice but to settle for a sad reality. Many look for relief through drugs, binge eating, or gossiping about others.

God promises in this aya that your life can be rekindled. He will heal your life if you develop faith and learn to do good. Faith is the foundation of a happy and fulfilling life.

Faith is often a misunderstood word. It has a political definition and a spiritual definition. It is political when it is used as a group identity. You introduce yourself by saying, "Hello, my name is Ahmad, and I am a Muslim." Or we hear in the news that in Lebanon there is conflict between the Christian and Muslim faiths. When people talk like this, they mean you belong to a group that has inherited a faith tradition. This is not the spiritual definition of faith, because there is no way you can inculcate the principles of faith merely by belonging to an ethnic group. You have to work on yourself for a long time to acquire faith.

Spiritual faith is a set of beliefs that liberate you from limitations and enhance your life's possibilities. In this aya, the word "faith" has this definition. It says: if you have faith, your life will turn around; you will have a good life. In all religious traditions, the purpose of faith is the same, but the principles are described differently. Let us discuss some of the attributes of faith taught by Prophet Muhammad.

The first belief is that God is benevolent. He has infused His spirit in you. You are blessed by so many gifts He has given you, so be grateful. The world He created is full of goodness. Nothing happens without God's permission, and He is most gracious and most compassionate. The difficulties you have are for a positive purpose. They are part of His plan to help you become better. To have faith is to know that God is near you and hears you. You can ask Him for help anytime, anywhere, and He will give you help at the right time. No barrier is too big to overcome when God helps you. Your past mistakes need not keep you down; you can have a fresh start and build a new life as you become grounded in faith.

To be pleased with what he had and to speak gratefully about it was a habit of Prophet Muhammad. To continuously ask for guidance, for protection, and for an increase in the good given to him was also a habit of Prophet Muhammad. Faith means knowing that our words have consequences. Every sentence we speak either expresses faith or it does not. Your life today has come out of what you said before, and what you think and say today will bring about your future life. A person of faith works to discipline himself to eliminate pessimistic thinking; he or she seeks to think thoughts of hope, appreciation, goodness, generosity, and speaks words that express these thoughts.

To have faith is to know that what we do to others always comes back to us. When I speak well of someone, the angels say: "May the same be true for you." When I speak badly of someone, the angels say: "May the same be true for you." Faith means we are careful not to harm anyone by either our words or actions. It also means that we never let go of an opportunity to help another. Faith means we make a serious effort to live with moral values. We learn to keep our promises, not deceive or manipulate. Honesty is the best policy, and we do not wish for others what we don't wish for ourselves.

There is healing in the remembrance of God. Make time every day for prayer, feeling grateful, speaking to God sincerely about your heart's desire. Asking for help and guidance heals your life.

God remembers those who remember Him. When you are by yourself, or waiting in a line, or riding a bus, remember that God is present and say to yourself, "God is with me. He guides me and protects me. I place my trust in Him, and His help is sufficient for me." As you say it again and again, it becomes true for you.

Regular evaluation of our thoughts and actions helps us acquire faith. It expresses the belief that your life can be better than it is. Every day, find time to think about what you did today. What are the positive steps you took today? What do you plan to do tomorrow? What will you do tomorrow to make it better than today? In what ways are you doing good, contributing to the people you know and don't know?

The people we spend time with influence us, so in order to become stronger in faith, we seek the company of people who have faith. You want to have friends who support you in your life journey, who are happy when you succeed, and who encourage you when you falter. You want to associate with people with whom you can share your experiences, your old and new thoughts, without being judged or criticized.

When the aya speaks of *who does what is good,* it refers to the good that you do for yourself and others. What you do to be in good health, to obtain knowledge, to succeed in your career is good because such activities strengthen you and increase your capacity to do good to others.

As a person turns the corner, develops faith, and begins to live with its values, help comes from above. There is a radical transformation in perception, attitude, and personality. You feel changed because you are thinking differently, managing your feelings differently, and acting differently. You have changed in profound ways. Because of these changes, you are able to do more and more for yourself and others. Your past limitations and mistakes become eclipsed. New avenues open to you based on where you are now. This is conveyed by the statement: *We shall give them their rewards according to the best they did.*

40

Banish Satan When You Read the Quran

Sura 16 Ayas 98–100

When you read the Quran, seek refuge with God from
Satan, the accursed.
Behold, he has no power over those who have developed
faith and place their trust in their Lord.
He has power over those who take him as their master,
and who thus ascribe to him a share in God's divinity.

In the human being, there is a simultaneous presence of good and evil.

Each of us has the ability to manifest love, compassion, generosity, fairness, forgiveness, restraint, truthfulness, courage, and the many other traits that we know are noble. These are also among the traits by which we know God; in fact, these are some of the divine names mentioned in the Quran. In as much as they are present in us, they represent the divine spirit in us.

On the other hand, we human beings have the tendency for arrogance, envy, greed, covetousness, laziness, deceit, and other harmful traits. These are the attributes of Satan described in the Quran and Hadith. In as much as they are present in any of us, they represent the evil spirit in us.

Religion is ancient. Its truths were taught originally to simple, unlearned people. With the passage of time, religion has become mixed up with superstition. The concept of Satan is an example of this tendency. The idea of a devil figure enchants many people, and there is an enormous amount of literature on the theology of evil, where Satan lives and possession of people by the devil and other outlandish topics. Most of it is meaningless and without basis in reality.

The word "satan" and the Arabic word *shaytan* are derived from the Semitic root *stn,* which has the meaning of opposing and obstructing. It represents the traits in the human being that oppose and sabotage his good intentions, his desire to manifest the divine spirit that is in him. Satan is not a person living somewhere; it is a symbol of beliefs that direct us away from our full potential.

Prophet Muhammad said, *"Satan flows in the blood of every person,"* which means satanic impulses are present in each of us. He also said, *"God, the Majestic, lives in the heart of every person of faith,"* which means that the divine attributes are within each person to the degree that faith has anchored in him or her.

When you or I read a text, there is an interaction between the words and what is in the mind of the reader. The words are just ink marks on the page. You assign a meaning to each word using your memory bank. You then string the words together and deduce a meaning, which is shaped by your motivation for reading the book.

These ayas ask us to be conscious of our motivation before we read the Quran. They ask us to seek God's help in banishing satanic tendencies that will mislead us.

The Quran is a revelation. Its each line is an aya, a sign to deeper truths. It is not to be read superficially or assertively. Because it points to profound truths using simple words, its language is often transcendental. It rewards those who are humble and patient in seeking the truth, and it repels those who are otherwise. It is said in Sura 2 Aya 26 about God's teaching in the Quran: *He misleads many thereby, and He guides many thereby; and with it He misleads those who are rebellious*.

Let us consider some of the limiting attitudes in people that block them from learning from the Quran:

Laziness: A person with a lazy frame of mind reads the Quran casually; he or she has low expectations from it. You believe that the Quran is a book of guidance, but you think there is not much of value in it. You read it to fulfill ritual obligations.

There are people who recite verses from the Quran in ritual prayer but don't stop to think about what the words mean and how they could relate to their lives. They don't care which verses they recite in the next prayer; they already forgot which ones they recited the last time they prayed. It is all the same to them. It is too much effort to figure out what all this means.

Impatience: The inability to grasp the fact that deep insight is not gained by cursory effort. Prophet Muhammad spent many years in contemplation before he received the first revelation, and then it took another twenty-three years for the revelation to be completed. But you started reading last month, and now you are ready to give a speech about it?

Selfishness: There are people who read the Quran to justify their social agendas. They have advantages over others, and they want to keep it that way by obtaining justification from the Quran.

Amina Wudud, in her book *Quran and Woman,* has documented that male commentators on the Quran have the tendency to justify the structure of the patriarchal society that gives advantages to men over women. She presents convincing evidence that most traditional commentaries are affected by this bias.

Over the centuries, autocratic rulers and kings have sought to justify their control of people by readings from the Quran. They hire scholars who interpret the Quran to support their masters. God is compassionate and merciful, but the king can be unfair and brutal, and this is justified by verses from the Quran.

Arrogance: The view that the Quran should support you as you are; that it can be used to prop up your current beliefs. You are confident you know what there is to know, and there is nothing significant outside your experience. The truth is your experience will change with time, and it is only a small shadow of Reality.

Another type of arrogance is based on nationalism or sectarianism. People read the Quran to create debating points, to prove that Muslims are better than Hindus, or the Sunnis are right and Ahmadies are wrong, etc. However, whether you are superior or inferior shows by the contribution you are making to the world; it is not determined by your label.

Rebelliousness: Some people read the Quran because they are angry with it. They want to prove it wrong. They are upset that so many people around the world believe it is the Word of God. Such people are unable to see wisdom in the Quran. They copy statements they think are irrational or promote violence or are not progressive and create propaganda. Such people have always existed, but they have no lasting impact. In every new generation, the number of people who look to the Quran for guidance increases.

The insight in these ayas has general applications. In any encounter you have with people or with events, the outcome for you is shaped by your state of mind. Before any undertaking, pause, compose yourself, and ask God for His help in bringing out what is best for you and others from this encounter. The help will come.

41

Advice on Food

Food is a daily choice, and people ask what guidelines there are on this topic in the Quran. Almost the same text appears at four places, in 2:172–173; 5:3–4; 6:146, and 16:114–115, with recommendations and prohibitions on eating. Ayas 114 and 115 from Sura 16 are given below as representative of this message.

So eat what God has provided you, lawful and wholesome, and be grateful for the favors of God if it is God that you serve.
God has forbidden to you only what has died of itself, and blood, and the flesh of swine, and anything offered up to other than God. But if anyone is compelled by necessity, without wanting to or being excessive, then God is very forgiving, very merciful.

In addition, there is a warning against over-eating in 20:81:

Eat of the wholesome things We provided for you, but not to excess, lest My anger descend on you. And whoever My anger settles upon has already fallen.

Most of the food practice in the Muslim culture has been in observing the prohibitions. But it is important to pay attention to other information in these ayas. To gain this perspective, we should note that being in good health is a very high priority in Islamic sharia. This originates from the extensive discussion of health, its value, and its preservation in the teachings of Prophet Muhammad. Having healthy habits was a part of the Prophet's religious discipline.

The following is a quotation from *The Life of Muhammad,* by Husein Haykal (1983), page 493:

"People knew that the Prophet never suffered from any serious ailment. Nothing had adversely affected his health throughout this period except a brief lack of appetite in the 6th year (after migration) and a little discomfort following his eating a bite of poisoned lamb in the 7th year. Furthermore, the rhythm of his life and the logic of his teachings always protected him against disease. He always ate little and satisfied himself with the barest and simplest necessities. His clothes and his house were always perfectly clean. The ritual of prayer and daily exercise which Muhammad observed as well as his sense of economy in the pursuit of pleasure, his refrain from indulgences of all kinds, and his general lack of concern for things of this world which kept him at a distance from them, but in communion with cosmic life and the secrets of existence—all these aspects of character protected him against disease and gave him good health."

In case we think that this was because he had good genes and inherited good health, you may recall that both his parents died in their twenties. The fact is that Prophet Muhammad chose to have healthy habits. His understanding of religion and its practice included health as an important component. Those who learned about Islam from him also became healthy people.

Please note that every aya in the Quran related to eating begins with the recommendation that we eat what is wholesome. The word *tayyib* written here as "wholesome" can also be translated as pure, or nourishing, or natural. This is, therefore, the most important teaching about food. Eat what is wholesome and pure.

It has been correctly said that our bodies are made up of what we eat, and, therefore, we owe it to ourselves to always eat wholesome and pure foods with high nutrition value. In the modern era, we have the benefit of knowing a great deal more about food products and their contents. People for whom health is a priority are conscious of this information. By the same token, we should avoid foods mixed with pesticides, artificial ingredients, and colors, and foods which have been subjected to industrial processing that depletes nutritional content.

Let us consider the prohibitions:

God has forbidden to you only the flesh of dead animals, and blood, and the flesh of swine, and anything offered up to other than God.

We can assume that these exclusions are to prevent damage to health. It is interesting to note what is known about this in modern data.

Flesh of dead animals: As soon as an animal dies, bacteria from its colon quickly invade the whole body, and the process of decay begins. An animal that has been dead for sometime is likely to be heavily infected, and therefore, a health risk.

Blood: Animal and human blood contain uric acid, which is one of the body's waste products and is a toxic substance. In normal body function, it is removed from the body through the kidneys in the form of urine. The traditional Muslim (and Jewish) method of killing an animal for food makes sure that blood is drained out. Accumulation of uric acid in the human body is related to gout, bladder stones, and also kidney disease. People with leukemia have an excessive concentration of uric acid.

Pork: Trichinosis is caused by eating undercooked meat infected with the larvae of a worm called Trichinella found commonly in wild meat-eating animals, but also in domesticated pigs. In days before refrigeration, people who consumed pork, especially if not thoroughly cooked, were vulnerable to this disease. We can assume that the susceptibility to this illness was high in the desert climate, where the heat causes rapid multiplication of bacteria. The symptoms of trichinosis infection are nausea, diarrhea, vomiting, fever, and abdominal pain. If the infection is severe, patients experience difficulty coordinating movements and have heart and breathing problems. In those cases, death can occur.

Note that the prohibitions are on certain types of meats. There are no prohibitions on plant food. It is well known that fruits and vegetables are the basis of any healthy diet. Because of the desert climate, Prophet Muhammad and his contemporaries had only very limited access to fruits and vegetables. Narratives in the Hadith show that the Prophet was aware that a meat-based diet is harmful for health.

If we pay attention to Prophet Muhammad's sayings and his personal habits, by far, the greatest emphasis is on avoiding over-eating, as is also seen in Aya 20:81:

Eat of the wholesome things We provided for you, but not to excess, lest My anger descend on you. And whoever My anger settles upon has already fallen.

This is illustrated by the narrative that the King of Ethiopia sent three physicians to Medina as a goodwill gesture to the Prophet. They stayed with the Prophet's community for three months but did not have an occasion to treat anyone. When preparing to depart, they expressed surprise at the absence of disease in the Muslim community. The Prophet said to them: *We are a people who do not eat when we are not hungry, and when we eat we do not fill ourselves.*

With the abundance of medical data we now have, it is common knowledge that eating more than what the body needs leads to obesity, which is correlated with a large number of diseases: high blood pressure, heart disease, diabetes, arthritis, several types of cancer, sleep apnea, abdominal hernias, varicose veins, gout, and other diseases.

Eat of the wholesome things We provided for you, but not to excess, lest My anger descend on you.

Note that God's anger is the same as the pain we suffer because of the choices we make.

Health is the chief underpinning of well-being. It is a measure of the energy we have to do what we want to do. Being healthy, we can help others. In serious conditions of poor health, we become dependent on others. Illness is often accompanied by pain, and prolonged illness results in emotional suffering for the patient and the family. We are fortunate to be alive in times when information, foods, vitamins, and exercise equipment are readily available for us to keep in good health. Let us make being healthy a high priority.

42

Abraham Was a Role Model

Sura 16 Ayas 120–123

Abraham was indeed a role model, obedient to God, true in faith, and he joined not gods with God.

He was grateful for the favors of God; He selected him and guided him to a straight path.

And We gave him the best in the world, and in the hereafter, he will be among the worthy.

So We have taught you this inspired message, "Follow the way of Abraham the true in faith, and he joined not gods with God."

It is revealing what these ayas say and not say about Abraham, the role model. They do not say what Abraham looked like, the language he spoke, his ethnicity, where he lived or when, or any of his circumstances. None of this is relevant to being a role model. The ayas describe the key traits of Abraham. He was true in his faith, and he was grateful for what was given to him. These are the attributes you need to be guided into an exemplary life.

You can read a book about Abraham or any other person you think is a role model. In order for it to be a book, it should have several hundred pages, so the author gives many details, real and imaginary, about the role model: descriptions of the town where he grew up, his appearance, what he saw in his travels, the people he met, and what they did to make an interesting story. Such details often distract people away from learning about the qualities that made this person special. As a result, people often make false associations. They come to the conclusion that in order to make a difference, "you have to be at the right place at the right time." Abraham was in the Middle East a long time ago. You are living now in a different place. So it is easy to say to yourself: "Everything is different now. The world is so much more complex, and there are so many things we have to deal with that did not exist in the world in which people like Abraham or Muhammad lived."

These ayas are asserting the opposite. Places, times, and circumstances have no power. They don't matter in what you can do with your life. Only faith in your attitude is what matters.

If you believe that you are not "at the right place," you are thinking that the place has power over you, that the place is like a god which determines what will happen to you.

You may think that people control your life. It can be your boss, a bully, a tribal leader; it can be an enemy; it can be your father, your mother, your husband, or your wife; it can be a king or president. In your mind, you have decided that this person has power over you; i.e., you have made this person into a god.

Some think they cannot have the best in life because

of their appearance, or their age or gender, or the school they went to. If you believe these things have power, then they do. These become gods in your life, and they keep you hemmed in.

The Quran says: stop thinking like this. Do not be intimidated by created things. Break out of the spell of the imagined gods. There is only one ultimate power, that of the true God who is near you, here and now. He responds to what you think and speak. Focus your attention on God and He will give you an exemplary life. Abraham is a role model because he did not join gods with God.

The process of enlightenment is given in a few short words in Aya 121:

He was grateful for the favors of God; He selected him and guided him to a straight path.

No matter who you are, where you are, and what the circumstances are, there are always some things in your life that you can feel happy about. Think of those and feel grateful for them. It can be that you have air you are breathing, and you have a mind with which you can think. Most people have many more gifts from God they can be thankful for.

There is a sequence this aya is teaching us. Learn to be grateful and you will become a special person. God will choose you as His friend, and He will show you the straight path in your life.

Note that learning to be grateful is the first step. It is an attitude that you can proactively choose. It makes you special because the majority of humankind has not reached this spiritual level yet. They are living in a state of complaining, being upset with what God has given them. The unhappiness is what dominates their feelings and blocks the flow of divine guidance.

There is an art to being grateful. In everything take note of what is good and feel happy about it. If you are healthy, acknowledge it and feel good about it. If you are sick, notice that you have medicines and feel happy about it. Notice any good quality in the people you know and feel good about it. Rejoice in the home you have, the clothes you wear, and the food you eat. Being grateful is a feeling. It is the habit of looking at the world as a place of benevolence. We connect with God through our feelings. The more deeply grateful you are, the greater the intensity with which God loves you. Your vistas expand, you meet better people, and better ways of life open for you.

Prayer rituals are organized around expression of gratitude. But because they are *rituals,* most people do them *ritually,* rather than spend time to experience the feeling of gratitude.

In *salat*, we have the phrase *rabbana lakal hamd*. It is an exclamation, "O my Lord, my Sustainer, to you I am so grateful!" In the books of Hadith, we read that when the Prophet Muhammad uttered these words, he would many times stay in the same posture for a long time, experiencing and internalizing the feeling. There are many people who do not experience gratitude in prayer, yet wonder why prayer does not work for them.

Al Fatiha is the standard prayer. Recall how the sequence in *Al Fatiha* is. It begins by expressing gratitude: *Alhamdu lillahi rabb-il-alameen,* "all praise and thanks are due to God the Sustainer of the worlds." It asks for guidance afterwards: *Ihdi nassirat- al -mustaqeem*, "guide us to the straight path." Expression of gratitude comes first and the request for guidance afterwards.

There is great confusion about what guidance to the straight path is and how you learn about it. It is a common misconception that guidance is what you read in a book by a religious scholar. Other people can tell you about guidance *they* have found. In history books, we read about the guidance that Prophet Muhammad received and how he lived by it. You will experience great confusion if you think you have to live as Prophet Muhammad did. Everyone is different and has his or her own unique path in life. Muhammad was a prophet, and his mission in life was that of a prophet. How can you live his life if you are a housewife, a school teacher, or manager of a supermarket? You need to find your own guidance, your own straight path to the best in life. Prophet Abraham, Prophet Muhammad, all the prophets tell us how they found *their* guidance. You can follow the principles they used to find guidance in *your* life. The principle is this: establish your connection with God by learning to be grateful and you *will* find guidance.

43

Convey Your Message with Wisdom and Patience

Sura 16 Ayas 125–128

Call people to the path of your Lord with wisdom and goodly exhortation, and argue with them in the most kindly manner. Your Lord knows best as to who strays from His path, and best knows who are on guidance.

And if you have to respond to an attack (in argument), respond only to the extent of the attack leveled against you; but to conduct yourselves with patience is indeed far better for you, since God is with those who are patient in adversity.

Endure, then, with patience, always remembering that it is none but God who gives the strength to endure adversity, and do not be sad over them and neither be distressed by the false arguments they devise.

Surely, God is with those who are conscious and are doers of good.

Prophet Muhammad spent many years in prayer and meditation, and God taught him the Truth. In this aya, he is being asked to invite others to the Truth about God. This commandment applies to us also. Although we may not have the complete understanding as Prophet Muhammad did, but there is a version of the Truth that you know and have experienced. There are things you know that if you convey to others, they will benefit from them. Your mission is to make the world better; you have been sent here as an agent of God. And if you do not help others with what you know, you are not doing your job. You are keeping what you know to yourself because of fear of criticism.

Prophet Muhammad was a shy person by nature. He had difficulty talking to others about what he had experienced. So for the first three years after he began receiving revelations, only a few people in his family knew. Then he received this message, that he must share the truth with others. He had to invite people to what he knew.

It is not easy to share your truths with others, because they already have beliefs they are convinced of. So if you tell someone that you have ideas about religion that are truly wonderful, they are likely to rebuff you. Therefore, we avoid such discussions because they can make us and others uncomfortable.

People have a tendency to invest their identity in their beliefs, so they tend to hold on to beliefs that are not true, simply because these are *their* beliefs.

These ayas teach us how barriers arise in conversations about religion and how to overcome them.

The first principle is that you always speak to people in a kind way, and if you are rebuffed, you do not lose your temper and become unpleasant. You do not want to speak in a way that would turn the other person off. Gentleness in manner and speech is a sign of strength. Kindness says what words alone cannot convey.

Another important piece of advice is that you detach your ego from this process. If you approach the situation from the point of view that you are the one in the know and you are going to set the other person on the right course by the force of your personality, you are leading with your ego and the other person is likely to be turned off. That is why the aya says, *"Your Lord knows best as to who strays from his path, and best knows who is on guidance."* It does not say to Prophet Muhammad in this situation, "Surely you are on the right path and the other people are misguided." It says to him: watch out, communicate in a way that is consistent with the path of the Lord and keep your own self out of it.

Also, although the person you are speaking to may benefit from your discussion, that individual also has some wisdom and guidance to share. You can learn from him also. You are more likely to make progress if you are respectful of how he or she sees life and are open to learning from that person.

And if you have to respond to an attack (in argument), respond only to the extent of the attack leveled against you; but to conduct yourselves with patience is indeed far better for you, since God is with those who are patient in adversity.

A discussion or debate can be useful, with each side making reasonable arguments, if it is conducted with a constructive spirit. If someone rejects you or insults you, do not take it personally. Respond in a dignified manner, focusing on the issues raised. We are asked to exercise self-restraint while arguing with people of other persuasions and never to offend against decency. Although you are permitted to respond if your integrity or motivation is attacked, these ayas make it clear that it is better for you to not retaliate and to bear unjust attacks with patience.

And there is the profound principle of faith stated in the last part of the aya that the help of God comes to those who are patient in a difficult situation.

This is the big payoff for us in this teaching. If you can overcome your hesitation and speak to other people about what you know is true, you are going to be in many tough discussions, and you will surely face adversity. But if you conduct yourself with dignity, you do not react to insults, you remain patient, then God will strengthen you. We have to remain conscious of the fact that it is God who is always in charge.

Endure, then, with patience, always remembering that it is none but God who gives the strength to endure adversity, and do not be sad over them, and neither be distressed by the false arguments they devise.

You made the effort to help another person, and the patience you learned in this exchange is God's gift to you. A deepening will occur in your spirit that is priceless as you persevere in any difficult situation.

And as you learn to be patient, remember that it is from God's grace that you are able to do so. Any spiritual growth that occurs is a gift from above, and we align ourselves to receive more by expressing gratitude for it.

It is a mistake to engage in negative thinking about why people do not follow your advice by expressing pity for their lack of understanding, by saying they are stupid, or how baseless their arguments are. There is good reason why the other person is how he or she is, and you are not helping them, or yourself, by feeling sorry for yourself or them.

Surely, God is with those who are conscious and are doers of good.

We are urged to keep the big picture in mind. It is not about winning an argument. It is always about being aware of the presence of God and helping others become likewise. Examine yourself to make sure that your motivation is to help people, to do good for them. Because this is the way of the Lord to which you are inviting them.

44

Think Carefully About What You Wish For

Sura 17 Aya 11
People ask for things that are bad as if they were asking for something good, for people are prone to be hasty.

This aya can also be translated as:
People pray for things that are bad as if they were praying for something good, for people are prone to be hasty.

This human quality is mentioned elsewhere also:
Man is a creature of haste (21:37)

It is a common observation that many people are unhappy with the work they do. They are in a career, and their livelihood is tied to their work, but they do not feel good about what they do all day long. How does this commonly experienced dilemma take place, and what is its solution? It usually arises with a sequence like this: You have just graduated from college, and you are excited about getting a job and making money. Someone tells you about a job opening, or you see an advertisement. You are eager to work and earn money, so you quickly apply and are hired. Later on, it dawns on you that you really did not choose this work carefully and you do not find it satisfying. But now you are experienced in this field and your income is tied to it so it is not easy to switch. The problem arose because you were in a hurry to get a job; you did not think ahead of time about what you would really like to do and why. If you had formed a clear idea about your preferred profession, you could have looked for work in it and in great probability found it.

Most of the unhappiness in people's lives can be traced back to the failure to think and plan ahead. This, then, forces them to make decisions in haste into choices which they later regret.

It is a truism to say that people are motivated in everything they do by the desire to gain pleasure and avoid pain. This aya speaks of those who are focused on immediate pleasure and are unwilling to think of its consequences in the long-term. A wise person has thought about his long-term plans and decided what will be a source of lasting happiness for him. He makes his daily choices according to his plan, and this often involves choosing activities that others may think to be less than pleasant at the moment.

We can focus on the pleasure we can have on different time horizons and this affects the choices we make every day. Consider a class of college students. Some are focused on the pleasure they can have with the entertainment this week; some are thinking about the pleasure from good grades after the final exam. Still others have a longer horizon and give attention to the quality of their degree when they graduate. A very few think about the positive purpose of their lives afterwards and how they can achieve it.

Prophet Muhammad has said, *"The results of actions are according to intentions, and everyone is given what he or she intended."* This means that God has made the world such that people get what they are looking for. Those who are focused on instant gratification do get it but miss out on long term happiness. Those who plan for the long-term are able to find what they are looking for, and they learn to be disciplined for this purpose.

Human beings are unique because we have the ability to think ahead and set goals for the future. We can ask ourselves, "What is the contribution I can make over the next thirty years?" "What will people remember me for?" "What will be the ultimate meaning of my life?" We can ask and find answers to such questions ahead of time and set our day-to-day priorities accordingly. We will then have the motivation for not falling for what is in front of us at a given moment.

The Quran urges people to think of their lives as a whole. It says that we will meet our Creator, and He will ask us what we did with the gift of life. Anyone for whom the total of the good they have achieved is greater than the harm they have done is a winner, and anyone for whom the reverse is true is a loser.

In order to make use of this advice, it is essential to have the habit of evaluating and measuring our lives. This is the basis of Umar ibn al-Khattab's saying: "Evaluate your life before it is evaluated." Self-evaluation is the regular practice of keeping your vision of yourself in front of you and aligning your present choices to move toward that vision. Each of us has multiple roles in life. You are a son or daughter, a brother or sister, a parent, a husband or wife, a friend, a colleague, a professional, and a community member. Conflicts often arise in relationships, and we are tempted to act in nasty ways in the rush of the moment because of the tendency to "be in haste." We need to think regularly about how we want to be remembered in these roles after we are gone. This will help us stay attentive when stresses arise in the day-to-day ups and downs in our relationships.

There are many attractions and distractions around us all the time. This is called *dunya* in the Quran. A person who has not decided on a purpose for his or her life is easily sucked into activities which provide brief pleasure but little or no lasting value.

Please note that most behaviors that people consider bad arise because we cannot control our tendency to be hasty.

A man who robs a bank or cheats in business is in a hurry to get money. He thinks it will take too long to get what he wants by legitimate means.

People gamble because they feel they can make money quickly without doing hard work.

Many people fall for the short-term pleasure of adultery and cause lasting damage to their marriage.

People crave junk food because it gives pleasure "in haste." They ask for it eagerly as if it were good for them. Similarly, people ask for more food when they are full and overeat, even when they know it will damage their health later.

A parent screams at a child because she thinks it would

take too long to teach good manners in a kind way.

We have all suffered from damaged relationships because we said things in anger we did not mean because the rush of emotion made us lose patience.

When people have serious disappointments, they engage in self-pity and say things that are obviously bad. For example, some people say, "I wish I was never born," or "I wish my life would end," "or "I wish I never had this child," and other self-damaging statements. This is because they are hasty in their understanding of what has happened, not knowing that every situation can be turned around through patient right action.

The temptation to lie, or cheat, or gossip, or act immorally in any way is because of the urge to get what we want quickly without thinking of the consequences later on.

The statement:

People ask for things that are bad as if they were asking for something good, for people are prone to be hasty

does not mean that we should never be in a hurry. It teaches us not to be impulsive. It asks us to think about the long-term consequences of what we are wishing in this moment.

45

Everyone Makes His or Her Own Path in Life

Sura 17 Ayas 13–15

And every human being's destiny have We tied to his or her neck. And We will produce for them an open book on the Day of Resurrection.

"Read your record. Sufficient is yourself today to read your account!"

Anyone who follows guidance does it for his own good; and anyone who goes astray does it to his own detriment; and no bearer of burdens bears the burden of another.

The insight given in these ayas is that everyone makes his or her own path in life. It is not what happens to you but what *you* do that makes the difference for you. Excuses are useless. No one else has the burden of your life.

Most people find this hard to believe because they see their life as dominated by others. You live with people, and you work with people, and some of them are stronger than you. And a great part of what you do depends on what others want. How can you make your own life?

There are many people whose lives are visibly controlled by others. A few commonly seen examples are:

A poor man or woman who works in a factory for ten hours a day whose supervisor is unsympathetic and tyrannical and there are no other jobs available.

A woman in a male-dominated society; the men believe it is their duty to control her for her own good.

You are kept down because your race or ethnicity is considered inferior by those who dominate the social order.

You are a single mother with children and little income.

You were born in a slum and did not receive any education.

You are married to someone who is demanding and domineering and you cannot afford to end the marriage.

You don't know anyone who can help you.

You were born disabled or were disabled in an accident or in war.

You have big financial obligations and little income so you work nonstop in a job that has no prospects for a better future.

These are daunting obstacles. But we all know of examples of individuals in such circumstances who defied the odds and made great lives for themselves. The main question is this: Are you going to break out of your circumstances and make a life greater than what everyone thinks is possible? It is possible, and it will happen if you are determined to make it happen. The Quran is a guidebook for those who want to make it happen. It records the inspirations received by Prophet Muhammad in his struggle to break out of his circumstances and create a new destiny for himself. He is a role model because he succeeded brilliantly, beyond what anyone could have imagined. He changed his destiny and those of others. As you succeed in taking charge of your life and master your own destiny, you will also uplift many others.

What can you do to take charge of your life and chart your own course? The first step is to believe in the truth taught in these ayas. Everyone's destiny is made by their own choices. No one bears another's burden. The reason for this is very simple. The greatest power a human being has is in his or her thoughts, and no one can control what you are thinking. Other people can control your physical conditions, they can punish you or put you in a prison, but they cannot enter your head and think your thoughts. God has given every human being the freedom to think his or her own thoughts because that is where the power resides. Others can say that I am a nobody, but it will not affect me unless I repeat it in my own mind. I have the power to say to myself, "I have a bright future." Others can see me as helpless, but I can believe God is helping me.

The first two ayas refer to a scientific fact. What I think and say and hear and feel and do is recorded in my mind. I may remember it, or it may fade from my conscious mind and become part of my subconscious. In either case, it becomes a part of who I am. It influences my perceptions and my decisions. I am the sum of all that I have accumulated in my mind so far, and this buildup is pushing me forward. It is guiding me toward my destiny.

What anyone else does, or does not do, does not affect me but what I think and say about others becomes part of me and affects me.

It is the same for everyone. What is in everyone's mind is an accumulation of what they have thought, said, heard, felt, and done, and this sum total of who they are is guiding their perceptions and decisions. The outcome of everyone's life is tied to what is in his or her mind.

We harm ourselves if we copy moral weaknesses in others; for example, be unfair if others treat us unfairly, or be dishonest if people around us are dishonest, or be lazy if we see lazy people, or become cynical, or angry, or revengeful if people in our family have these attitudes, or have small aims if people around us think small, or be without hope if people around us feel hopeless about the future. We can choose our thoughts differently. It is difficult, but it is possible, and it is crucial.

In order to take charge of your thinking, it is very important to become aware of how you think at present. Find time every day for introspection. Sit in a quiet place and pay attention to the movie that is playing in your mind. When we are quiet, thoughts and pictures from the subconscious float up and reveal parts of us we are not aware of.

A lot of what you find in your thoughts is about yourself and people important to you. Thoughts within us can be happy, encouraging, and hopeful, but there are other thoughts that are unhappy, fearful, and discouraging. We can repeat and strengthen the thoughts that support us and let go of those in which we see ourselves as weak.

There can be recurring images of people who have hurt us deeply. There is a renewal of the raw energy of pain that can overcome us every time their image appears in our thoughts. We can let go of such painful feelings by recalling what these ayas teach us. What the other person did is around his or her neck. I want to free myself from this experience by thinking kindly about them and everyone else. We can learn to forgive people who have hurt us. Forgiving someone often appears difficult because we feel that we are letting the person off the hook for the wrong that he or she did. But forgiving, in reality, helps the forgiver. It helps to heal the wound that is within me by erasing the recurring images of the hurt. It stops the painful movie from playing again and again and creating havoc in your feelings and draining your energy.

Another step toward taking charge of your life is to set high goals for oneself. What do you want your life to be like? Where do you want to live, what do you really want to do, how much money do you want to have? What would you like to accomplish if you knew God is helping you? Then remember that God helps you every time you ask for His help. It is said in Sura 2 Aya 186, *If My servants ask about Me, behold I am near, I respond to everyone who calls, whenever he or she calls, let them then respond to Me and have faith in Me, so that they may find the right way.*

It is a lot easier to take charge of your life if you associate with positive people and disassociate from those who like to gossip, complain, and backbite. In ancient times, travel was difficult and people were forced to interact daily only with those who lived nearby. But now in any town we can go to people who would uplift our thinking. In the book of Bukhari, Prophet Muhammad is quoted as saying, *"It is better to sit alone than in company with the bad; and it is better still to sit with the good than alone. It is better to speak to a seeker of knowledge than to remain silent; but silence is better than idle words."* Human beings are strongly influenced, both consciously and unconsciously, by people they spend time with. The goals we set for ourselves are heavily shaped by the people we talk to regularly. Whether we have goals or choose to drift is also influenced by the company we keep. Another form of company each of us chooses is by what we watch on television, the messages in the books we read, and in the music we listen to. Every day we choose the influences that enter our minds and shape our future.

46

Seek to Create Permanent Value

Sura 17 Ayas 18–21

If anyone seeks transitory things, We hasten to him what We will of them, to whom We wish: then We bring him hell where he is miserable and unwanted.

And if anyone seeks for the future and strives for it, as it should be striven for, and has faith, his effort is greatly appreciated.

To everyone We give, to this one and that one, from the gifts of your Lord; and the gifts of your Lord are not restricted.

See how We make some of them excel over others; but the hereafter is of higher order and greater in merit.

After a life lived over fifty, sixty, or seventy years, there is a net result. All the years of coming and going, talking and listening, eating and sleeping boil down to a net outcome. Those who spend their time consumed by the desires of day-to-day living find that their life adds up to little or nothing. But those who take a long view, plan for the future, and strive for their plans, can build something of permanent value. Such people are pleased with what they have achieved. Everyone will get some of what he or she is looking for, some more and some less. Those who are looking for small things will get some of them; those who are looking to make an important difference will find some of it. We make the choice by what we seek.

Within each human being lays a deep desire to live a life that will have lasting significance. This is felt very clearly when we are young, but most people give up on it as time passes. There are many forces acting on us that focus our attention on the transitory needs. There is the struggle for survival. Most people work for a living, and this leaves them little time or energy to think of the long-term meaning of life. There is great pressure on us from advertising to keep us busy consuming more and more products that give us only temporary comfort and pleasure. Clever people bombard us with messages to convince us that we should spend our lives working harder, making more money so we can buy more of what they sell. There can be negative pressure from your family. You may have lofty goals for the future, but your spouse, your children, or your parents may be absorbed in the ordinary humdrum of life. These ayas are an appeal to people to escape such traps and recognize the great gift of life, because within each human being is the potential to do great things if he or she would have faith and seek to do it.

No matter what our circumstances are, God has given us the power to rise above them. The greatest resource is in our thinking. You can take the easy way to think like everyone else, or you can choose to think better thoughts. People around you can be pessimistic, but you can decide to be optimistic; others can be cynical, but you can be hopeful; people around you can be self-centered, but you can plan to make a positive difference in the world. It is not easy, but it is possible. Your superior intentions will inevitably bring you in contact with people who think like you, and you can have a life different from those you started out with.

Everyone has a unique combination of intelligence, feelings, and personality. These talents can be nurtured to become formidable forces of constructive change. Many people doubt their ability to live a life of significance because they feel they are different from those who are famous or successful. But no two people are alike, and everyone can make a difference with what they have. If you choose work that pleases and inspires you, your talents will expand, and if you make the intention of living not only for yourself but also to make a contribution to others, your life will create significance and impact.

These ayas do not ask us to live in poverty or to shun the world. They ask us to look at life in its totality, to make a determined effort to create permanent value out of it. You can live well and enjoy life every day, and also have resources and goals of making a major contribution.

The message in these ayas is the essential theme of the Quran, and it is repeated frequently. God has created you as His agent in the world and given you the mission of making it a better place. When you meet God after your life is over, He is going to take account. He is going to ask you to explain what you did with the gift of life. All the teachings in the Quran about faith in God, prayer, remembrance, and morality are aimed at helping us to succeed in the final accounting by achieving a life of significance and positive purpose during our stay on the earth. The tenets of faith are taught so you can be free of fear in the struggles that you will encounter in moving higher. We should remember God often so that we get to know that His help is nearby, and with His aid, great changes are possible. We should pray to seek God's help in achieving our purpose. The rules of morality are taught so we can be upright and strong in the effort to transcend our circumstances. The Quran presents Prophet Muhammad as a role model for people. He was born in limiting circumstances but made a lasting contribution using the principles of faith, prayer, and action.

On one occasion, Prophet Muhammad used these words to convey the lesson that we should value the gift of life:

Seize the opportunity of the five (gifts)
before the five (calamities come to you):
your youth before old age;
your health before disability;
your wealth before lack;
your free time before preoccupation, and
your life before death.

Let us consider how hell is described in Aya 18:

If anyone seeks transitory things, We hasten to him what We will of them, to whom We wish: then We bring him hell where he is miserable and unwanted.

Hell is the state of being miserable and unwanted. Contrary to popular notions, it is not a hot place in the sky where people are being burned. The feelings of misery and dejection, of being unwanted and ignored, grip people when they perceive that life has passed them by and nothing worthwhile has come out of it. The time they had and the money they made were spent chasing after things that don't matter. Life without a lasting purpose becomes an internal hell of emptiness. If you have lived only for yourself, you end up only with yourself—unwanted and ignored by others.

47

Be Good To Your Parents, Especially When They Are Elderly

Sura 17 Ayas 23–25

Your Lord has decreed that you serve none but Him and that you be good to parents. If one or both of them become elderly in your life, do not say to them a word of disrespect, nor shun them, but speak to them in kind words.

And lower to them the wing of humility through mercy and say: "My Lord! bestow on them your mercy as they nurtured me when I was little."

Your Lord knows what is in your hearts: If you are righteous, verily He is most forgiving to those who turn to Him again and again.

On the surface, everyone agrees with this advice to be kind to aging parents, but a large number of people find it very difficult to act upon it. Whether you are able to be good to your parents or you neglect them, or abuse them, has huge consequences for your own happiness. It is, therefore, important to understand the psychological and spiritual factors involved in this question.

I have noticed that if a baby is present in a social gathering, then many people come forward to adore it, to say how cute and delightful he or she is. Many want to hold the baby. But we usually do not see a similar expression of excitement for an elderly person in the same room. No one seems to think that an old person is cute. Some who are dutiful express kindness, but many ignore the old person. The bias against the aged is instinctive. It is not limited to our feelings toward fellow humans. You may have noticed that most people consider kittens to be cute and lovable, but not old cats. When there is a baby animal in the zoo, people gather to express their delight at the lovely creature but ignore an old member of the same species who may be nearby.

This asymmetry in our attitudes toward the very young and the very old is rooted in the struggle for survival during evolution. Through most of the existence of life on earth, resources were scarce. The young represented the chances of the group to continue to exist and, thus, were given special attention; they had to be protected and nurtured. The old already did what they could for the species and were no longer of use. So, they were not paid attention to.

If we objectively look at the characteristics of the very young and very old, we find many similarities. Both are frail and need help with their needs. Both may need assistance with feeding. Both need protection and cannot be left alone when they go out. Both can be irrational and throw temper tantrums. But because of our instinctive bias, we take care of the needs of our children cheerfully, yet find it very difficult to do the same tasks for elderly people.

The instruction in these ayas is to go higher than the animal-like conditioning of the past. We are being asked to take care of old parents, to meet their needs, to absorb their irrational behavior—as they did the same for us when we were little.

Notice that the aya is not asking us to *obey* our parents, but to be *kind* to them. This is an important distinction. Each of us is to make our own lives with our own decisions after we become adults. When we were children, we were dependent on our parents' authority, and because of this early association, we have the tendency to continue to seek our parents' approval in our decisions. Many times, parents find it difficult to let go of the habit of trying to supervise their children's lives, even after they have become independent. It is healthy to seek advice from people we consider wise, including our parents, but we must resist the easy temptation of obeying their preferences automatically.

Like any other spiritual principle, the advice given here has a personal benefit. The moral principle exists because it has advantage for us, although it requires a sacrifice from us first. It is very likely that you will be old and frail one day. The way you deal with your parents now is observed by your children. They are likely to model your behavior. Their attitude toward you when you are old is going to be influenced by what they see you doing now with your parents.

Looked at another way, this advice is about balancing your account with your parents. The Law of Compensation is real and it exacts retribution, one way or another, if we take more and give less. The reality is that I am here alive and in good shape because my parents went to infinite troubles to nurture and protect me when I was little. None of us remembers our infancy to know the magnitude of their favors to us. It is narrated in Hadith that an old woman who lived in Yemen was frail but she wanted to fulfill her life-long desire to go to Mecca for pilgrimage. Her son could not afford to hire conveyance so he carried her on his back and walked the five hundred miles to Mecca and carried her through the rites of Hajj. He chanced to meet Prophet Muhammad and asked him if he had done enough for his mother. The Prophet replied to him by saying: "You did not fully compensate her even for the months she carried you around when she was pregnant with you".

Kindness to parents many times requires supporting them financially. It is possible that they will have a reduced income in their senior years. You have to decide whether you are comfortable with living at your high level of well-being, and your parents living at a much lower level.

Aya 23 begins by saying: *Your Lord has decreed that you serve none but Him and that you be good to parents.*

Serve only God and be good to your parents. These are one and the same in this context. When we act out of our higher impulses of love and generosity, we are serving God. Deep inside our conscience, everyone knows what the right thing to do is. When we carry it out, we serve God. On the other hand, if we are swayed by lower impulses of selfishness and limitation, we serve other than God. Being consistently kind to and caring for your elderly parents who may be needy and irrational requires us to act out of our higher selves. If a rude comment by a parent provokes you and you retaliate in kind, you are working from your ego and not your conscience.

Your Lord knows what is in your hearts: If you are righteous, verily He is most forgiving to those who turn to Him again and again.

The advice of kindness to parents, being always patient and not speaking to them harshly, demands a great deal of effort on our part. Most people are busy with family life and careers when their parents become old. The emotional, physical, and financial needs of the parents appear like an extra burden on your time and resources when it seems you don't have any to spare. You and your spouse may have strong disagreements on how to take care of needy parents. Your commitment to do the right thing will be tested again and again. But if you are able to follow through with the qualities of your higher self, there are tremendous rewards for your moral and spiritual strength. Many of your limitations will disappear and you will gain greatly in how you view yourself and how others view you.

48

Human Life Is Sacred

Sura 17 Aya 33

And do not take any human life—which God has made sacred—otherwise than in the pursuit of justice.

Hence if anyone has been slain wrongfully, We have given the heir authority (to demand retribution or to forgive): but even so, let him not exceed the bounds of equity in retributive killing; for verily, he is supported.

The defining principle is described in the opening statement: *do not take any human life*. Human life is sacred, and it should be protected.

The penalty for homicide is termed *qisas* in the Quran, described in Sura 2, Aya 178. The principle of *qisas* gives the family of the victim the right to demand retribution or to forgive the life of the murderer and to accept monetary compensation instead.

The last part of the aya warns against feelings of revenge.

It is useful to recall the social-historical context in which the aya was revealed. In the tribal Arab society, there was no civic government and no legal framework. A person's protection derived from his affiliation with his tribe. If someone from Tribe A was murdered by someone from Tribe B, then the chief of Tribe A considered it his duty to avenge this death by killing one or more of the members of Tribe B. Extreme emotions of avenging tribal honor came into play and excesses were committed in revenge, which resulted in spirals of killing which sometimes lasted for generations.

This type of group behavior still persists in some parts of the world where societies have continued to have a tribal structure, and the value of individual human life is not acknowledged.

In many other parts of the world, society has evolved past a tribal framework and has established common law based on protecting the rights of the individual, and there are courts for justice. In many places, the death penalty is mandated for those convicted of murder.

The principle of *qisas* offers a less gruesome alternative. The family of the victim can choose to be compensated financially and forego the revenge killing of the murderer.

In still other parts of the world, such as countries of northern Europe, there is greater spiritual growth, and society as a whole has gone beyond the need for revenge. In those countries, the practice of killing a person in retribution—the death penalty—has been discontinued. This is a manifestation of the highest aims of this aya. Comparisons of different societies have shown that violence breeds violence. Those societies that have given up the death penalty have fewer crimes of murder than those where killing in retribution of killing continues.

49

Leave Alone What Is Irrelevant

Sura 17 Aya 36

And do not concern yourself with anything of which you have no knowledge: verily, the use of your hearing, your seeing, and the feelings in your heart—all of them—will be questioned.

God has placed His spirit in the human being. The spirit expresses itself through our faculties of seeing, hearing, thinking, speaking, and feeling. These faculties have great power. Everything we accomplish, and everything anyone ever accomplished, was by using these faculties. Some people have used them to create better lives for themselves and others, while others used them in ways that created misery for themselves and others. A day will come when your life on the earth will be over and you will meet your Creator. He will ask you, "I gave you powerful tools of creation. What did you do with them?"

This aya advises us not to squander our faculties. Our attention is attracted to many things, most of which we know little about and which have no use to us. Spend your time and energy in achieving a positive purpose. Leave alone what is irrelevant.

When you are in college, you spend four years reading, writing, and hearing about a particular subject. Your energies become concentrated in that direction, and you receive a diploma certifying you are knowledgeable about that particular specialty. Most people use this knowledge to make a living. Your success in college depends on your ability to concentrate and keep yourself away from distractions. Those who can concentrate on their studies have little time for diversions and are at the top of the class. Those who spend much of their time on distractions irrelevant to their purpose are at the bottom of the class.

Your success in life also depends on your ability to concentrate on what you should be doing and avoid distractions.

Every aspect of life can be made better. Your health can be better, your relationships can be better, your work productivity can be better, your finances can be better, your prayer life can be better. Improvement begins by establishing goals for your life in order to be better in specific ways. Then get busy with collecting information on how you can realize your goals. Talk to people who have achieved what you want to achieve. Read about people who have accomplished what you want to accomplish. You then have no time for things which are not relevant to your purpose.

When we work toward a goal, we find that it is an uphill walk. Success comes slowly and unevenly. There are disappointments, and there are long patches of frustration. Successful people learn how to keep their motivation alive when they are frustrated. Weak people give in to distractions and become sidetracked.

An expert is someone who has applied his mind to a particular topic with greater attention than others. There have been people who developed extraordinary discipline and focused their energies on their chosen purpose so exclusively that they are called geniuses. Newton and Einstein concentrated their minds on learning how the physical world works. Mozart and Beethoven devoted their energies to creating beauty through music. Buddha, Jesus, and Muhammad concentrated their energies on learning about the spirit. All the great achievements of civilization came about because someone decided to expend his or her energy for a particular purpose. Those people became so focused they lost interest in the distractions and amusements that occupy the minds of most people.

On the other hand, people who do not have positive purpose are looking for distractions to fill their time. They are eager to talk about people and things of which they have little or no information. This is seen frequently at social gatherings. It is fascinating to see two people exchange opinions about a famous person about whom neither of them knows anything with certainty. Similarly, many people are fond of offering opinions on subjects with which they have little experience.

Politics is a topic of popular interest. There is a difference between those who gossip about politics and those who make a difference. We do not do any good to ourselves or to our country by repeating hearsay about public figures. Those who want to make a positive contribution join with like minded others in concerted political action to change society in their preferred direction. Such people have little time for idle talk.

Hearing and speaking, thinking and feeling are faculties of the spirit, and they have magical powers. Everything a human being pays attention to in a sustained manner expands. When we think of something again and again, we find more and more of it in our lives. This power of the spirit works both ways. Those who have discovered positive uses for their faculties find that success becomes easier and easier as time passes. But also, those who live without a purpose and fill their time with gossip and vain talk become engulfed in expanding feelings of futility and powerlessness. Most people think that gossiping is considered bad because it hurts the person we are gossiping about. The reality is that it causes greater damage to the person who is gossiping by draining their God-given energy into low channels and making them blind to the lofty stations that could be possible for them.

There are so many things we can talk about, and there are so many ways we can spend our time. Successful people focus their energies on achieving their goals. Their attention is not available to wander to miscellaneous attractions around them.

50

Speak only the Best

Sura 17 Aya 53

And say to My servants to speak only what is best: For Satan does sow dissension among them: for Satan is openly an enemy to people.

All of us have been in situations where there are quarrels and discord among people. It can be experienced in a family, a business, an association, or a congregation. Dissension begins when someone starts to speak ill of another. If the other responds in kind, bad feelings multiply. If it continues, there can be deep hurt and lasting antagonism.

The same dynamic occurs in personal relationships. It can involve your spouse, siblings, parents, neighbors, or colleagues. The basis of hostility is that someone starts to blame or insult another.

This aya advises us to choose the best words. We will then have strong relationships. Any purpose we have is achieved with the help of other people. The purpose can be to raise a family, to run a business, or build an organization. Its success depends on how people feel about each other. There can be many sources of friction or suspicion, but we have to take the responsibility of creating harmony. You have to actively foster harmony and good feelings by using good words to the people around you.

But what should I do when I see someone making wrong decisions and doing harm? Shouldn't I talk about it? Blaming, condemning, or attaching bad labels to people is not a solution. It makes the other person defensive. They either internalize their anger or are provoked to retaliate. A wise person finds other ways to mend the situation. We can try to understand the other person better and connect with them in a friendly way so that our dialogue can be constructive. It frequently happens in a close relationship that we share the same goals but think about how to achieve them differently. Trying to approach the other person in a constructive manner is often difficult. It does not produce results quickly, but it eventually yields some positive results. On the other hand, venting your anger gives a quick sense of relief but results in long-term damage.

This aya is asking us to be conscious of what we say. Words have consequences. Each of us has a habitual way of speaking, and it is a mixture of good and bad. Do not be in the automatic mode of speaking. Choose to use better words in your speech and your life will gradually but surely change for the better.

We have the power to change other people through the words we speak. Speak ill of another person, and he will sooner or later turn against you. Speak consistently well of the other person, and he will become your friend. In this you have the power to decide how other people will be toward you. Relationships work according to this principle, even if the speaking is done in the absence of the person you are speaking of.

This aya tells us about the nature of Satan.

And say to My servants to speak only what is best: For Satan does sow dissension among them.

Satan is the tendency within us to see people in less than the best way. Prophet Muhammad said: *laziness is from Satan*, and it is lazy and easy to be suspicious, to find fault, and to blame. The reality is that the spirit of God is in each human being. Compassion, courage, generosity, magnanimity, forgiveness, and all other divine traits are present in each person. These qualities may be dormant, but they are embedded in human nature. Your task in life is to help bring out these attributes in the people you know. When you get to know anyone closely, no matter what others say about him, you realize that he is trying to do his best according to what he thinks is possible. You can help him by assuming the best about him and ascribe the best to him in your thinking and in your conversation.

Self-sabotage is a big issue for most people. They make plans to make their life better, but they are not able to follow through. They take a few steps and then they inexplicably do things that sabotage their plans. In psychology, this phenomenon is called the "Divided Self"; that is, a person has dissension within himself because one side of him wants to succeed, but the other side of him wants to fail.

The root cause of self-sabotage is found in the words the person speaks to himself. People are used to putting themselves down. There is a division because at one level, they have a high opinion of themselves. But at a different, deeper level, they have a low opinion of their abilities, which is expressed in the words they speak.

Many times, self-criticizing statements are spoken subconsciously. Sometimes, they are spoken when people are tired or sleepy. These words were implanted in their minds when they were little in the criticisms they received from their parents and others. These ill-spoken words are written deep in their minds. The individual keeps repeating them automatically, and in this way, continues to self-sabotage himself.

You can remedy self-sabotage by using the advice given in this aya. Speak only the best about yourself so you can heal the dissent within you. Overcome any urge to make limiting statements about yourself. When self-criticisms appear in your mind, take note and replace them with self-approving statements.

Note that this aya teaches us to speak *only* the best. This gives us two rules of wisdom. First, try to speak better words than you are used to speaking. Improve your vocabulary. Do not be satisfied with the lukewarm words you are accustomed to. Second, if you find yourself in a situation where you cannot think of something good to say, then it is better to say nothing. Resist the temptation to say something bad in reaction to what others are saying or doing just to keep the conversation going.

The advice in this aya will transform anyone's life that uses it. But it takes a lot of effort over a long time to benefit from it. Knowing about it, or thinking about it is not enough. The way we speak is deeply rooted in our personalities. You have to pay attention to how you feel and how you speak. Daily, oppose the tendency to criticize yourself and others. Find new words that are better to describe yourself and others. It takes time for this change to be internalized. But if you persist and are patient, you will overcome the patterns that sabotage your relationship with yourself and others.

51

Dignity of Man

Sura 17 Aya 70

Indeed, We have conferred dignity on the children of Adam, carried them over land and sea, provided for them nourishment out of good things, and endowed them far above most of Our creation.

It is a privilege to experience life as a human being. Each of us has been gifted with intellect, imagination, and feelings. We can observe, remember, search, plan, calculate, and build. Although many people do not recognize it as such, these are resources of immense power. The systematic use of these faculties has empowered human beings to invent devices that allow them to navigate over land, sea, and air, and people have made countless other inventions that have increased their power.

This aya points to an important spiritual reality: the intrinsic worth of man because of his great potential. Everyone knows this truth instinctively. For this reason, the most important need of a human being is to feel valued, to be respected, and to be honored. You do not have to accomplish anything to have self-worth; it has already been gifted to you by God. The greatest service we can do for a person is to help him or her feel valued, respected, and honored. On the other hand, we do great damage when we put someone down—yourself or somebody else—in their presence or in their absence. There is great unhappiness in the world today because many people do not feel valued and honored. To recognize that each human being has great value is a mark of spiritual maturity.

To actively work to establish the dignity of a human being is a spiritual path. We do it by not only speaking well of the other person and by acting with good manners but also by helping resolve his or her problems, by enabling them to do more, by helping them discover their potential. In a Hadith reported in Bukhari, Prophet Muhammad said: *"What actions are most excellent? To gladden the heart of human beings, to feed the hungry, to uplift the afflicted, to lighten the sorrow of those who are sad, and to remove the sufferings of those who have been hurt."*

Low self-esteem is a deviation from the truth in this aya and, therefore, is a source of great unhappiness. From early childhood, we become conditioned to seek acceptance by others. As we grow up, popular standards of success are presented to us again and again by people around us and by television and movies. Many reach the conclusion that their value is determined by conforming to the standards set by others. Low self-esteem and insecurity are the inevitable results.

In every society, a particular type of face or body type is considered good-looking. If you are different from the popular ideal, you get the feeling that you are inferior and, therefore, doomed to unhappiness. This is an incorrect way of thinking. The fact is that everyone has a unique appearance. The criteria of good looks are different in different societies and in different times. The way God has made you and me has great value in its uniqueness. My happiness depends on how I think about myself and not on what others say.

Similarly, there are socially accepted standards of material success and professional accomplishment. Many people who fall short of popular notions of success feel that they have failed in life and, thus, are not of much worth. Such comparisons are incorrect because they are based on arbitrary criteria. Each human being has a unique mixture of talents and handicaps, and life unfolds differently for everyone. The responsibility of each of us is to learn and do our best to make life better, but the results are determined by many factors, some, of which, are out of our control. There is satisfaction if we use the talents given to us to make life better for ourselves and others, and we leave the world better than we found it.

In order to live by the wisdom of this aya, we should act in ways that recognize our self-esteem, irrespective of our circumstances. Train yourself to behave with poise, to walk like a dignified person, and to talk like a noble person. Do not use words of inferior meanings and never use foul language. You create your self-esteem by how you conduct yourself when you are alone. Always be aware that the way you dress, sit, stand, talk, or eat, even when you are by yourself, makes a statement about the value you place on yourself.

God has infused His breath in the human being and, therefore, each person has great worth. In the present stage of the world's spiritual development, many people still evaluate each other by external criteria of wealth and appearance. Those who are poor or diseased or come across as "different" are looked down upon by many. To establish a society in which each person's value is recognized is the main work of civilization. This is achieved when everyone has the same rights and the same opportunity. To make a deliberate effort to realize this goal is the task God has assigned to each of us.

There are people who are not aware of the wisdom of this aya and consider the human being as limited or evil. Some place the human being in the same category as animals. The scientist-author James Lovelock writes in his book *The Revenge of Gaia: Earth's Climate Crisis and the Fate of Humanity*, "As individual animals we are not so special, and in some ways the human species is like a planetary disease...." He is pessimistic that human civilization can survive problems caused by industrial development. Such statements ignore the great ingenuity of the human being. It is true that people often create problems by pursuing short-term interests, but human beings have the capacity to solve the problems they have created. The present state of the environment is a result of successes in overcoming poverty and hunger that plagued humanity in the past. When we solve one problem, a new set is bound to arise. But human beings have been given the resourcefulness to rise above the problems they create.

52

Continuous Prayer

Sura 17 Aya 78

Keep up prayer from the time when the sun declines till the darkness of night, and keep the recitation at dawn: for, behold, the recitation at dawn is indeed witnessed.

The traditional interpretation of this aya is that it is an injunction about the ritual prayers: in the afternoon, at sunset, at night, and in the morning. But read the aya again, or another translation of it, and notice it presents a broader view of prayer. It does not specify particular times but asks us to keep up prayer during the day and the night, to stay mindful of the reality that God is with you.

The wisdom of this aya has become inaccessible to people who believe prayer is only if you follow an elaborate ritual with proper washing before it, and you need a mat to pray on. You then say to yourself, "I cannot pray because I am at work during the day."

Let us recall that prayer is remembrance of God any way we do it, and we gain strength by remembering

God's favors and asking for His help every time we do it. Interrupting your workday with short periods of prayer prevents you from feeling overwhelmed and burdened with anxiety, and it keeps you in touch with the larger reality. There are many ways of remembering God. You can find one that is meaningful to you. Some examples are as follows.

Find a quiet place where you can sit down and say your words of prayer during a break from work.

If you don't relate to traditional prayer, find a few minutes away from work, take a few deep breaths, and release feelings of frustrations and the sense of being overwhelmed that have accumulated. Stay quiet and experience calm.

Write a list of things in your life you are happy with and keep it with you. Bring this list out and read it. Expressing gratitude is prayer. Do this several times every day and more and more happiness will flow into your life.

Write a page describing what you want your life to become. Write about ways in which you want to be better. Say what contribution you want to make to your family, your community, your work, and to the world. Read this page. This is your supplication. Read it several times a day, and in due time, what you wrote will come into your life.

There are people who experienced fulfillment of their prayers. They know that prayer is a way of overcoming obstacles and creating miracles. Such people experiment with prayer and find the type of prayer that helps them. As they progress, they feel a oneness with God, they receive guidance, and they achieve what they want with little effort. Such people pray all the time. This aya is asking us to become like these people.

In learning to pray well, you have to reform your view of

what God is like. This is an issue with many people because when they were children, they were taught to fear God. If the word God creates fear in you, it is likely you utter words of prayer in a fearful manner. Your prayer then produces more fear in you. Recall the Hadith Qudsi: *"whatever My servant assumes of Me, that is how I am to him, and I am with him as he remembers Me."* That is, God will manifest in your life as you have imagined Him. First, do the work to create a benevolent view of God in your mind. Convince yourself that God is beneficent, loving, forgiving, always responds to your requests, never abandons you, is always to be trusted, and does not produce any circumstance that does not help you.

In a Hadith reported in the Book of Muslim, Prophet Muhammad gave this advice: *"Create the feeling in you that God is looking at you in the most loving way."* If you have difficulty imagining God looking at you, you can remember that people who have looked at you in a loving way were sent by God; they are the agents of God. This includes your mother and father, your husband or wife, brother or sister, friends or strangers, your pet cat or dog, everyone who has made you felt loved. The important difference is to know and believe that you are loved—you are loved by people and by God—you are the beloved of God. Recall and repeat in your mind images of people looking at you in a loving way, and in time, you will become deeply convinced of this. It will then be easy for you to look at others in a loving way—your father and mother, your husband or wife, your brother or sister, your friends, strangers, and animals. You will become an agent of God's love for His creatures.

Let us consider the second part of the aya: *keep the*

recitation at dawn: for, behold, the recitation at dawn is indeed witnessed.

Although God is always present and is everywhere, all times of the day and all places are not equal in their efficacy for prayer.

Every place has its own spiritual energy. For example, if you watch a lot of television, there is energy of noise and conflict in your TV lounge. You will not find it easy to experience peaceful thoughts in that room. It is preferable that you assign a separate place in your home for prayer. As time passes, this place will accumulate the spiritual energy of your prayer, and it will enhance your prayer. Places where there is unspoiled nature are conducive to prayer. Places where a lot of people have prayed have accumulated spiritual energy. Examples of these are mosques, churches, and temples; your prayer is enhanced in such places. If you visit the Ka'bah, you can perceive a powerful electric feeling near it which is the accumulated energy from the millions and millions of people who have prayed there, including Prophets Muhammad, Abraham, and Ismail.

Similarly, each time of the day has its own force. Dawn, the time before sunrise, is a very auspicious time for prayer. The creation awakens at this time. Plants, birds, insects, animals in the forests all were dormant during the night and renew their consciousness at dawn. This releases a great impulse of spiritual energy and raises your consciousness at this time.

Many people in modern urban cultures have developed habits that have deprived them from experiencing the magic of the dawn hour. Learn to be awake at dawn and you will gain tremendous power over your life. If you find it impossible to rise early at the present, make an intention to do so, think about it often, pray about it, and write about it in your journal. You will find that you will eventually change and what was previously difficult becomes easy, and you *will* awaken early.

The literal meaning of the word Quran is recitation, and that is how it has been translated in the aya above. Recitation is something you say to yourself again and again. Your recitation at dawn is witnessed by the creation and contains great power in shaping your life.

There is power in becoming aware of your recitation, that is, the sentences you say again and again every day. Take a few moments at the end of the day, think back, and recall what sentences you spoke several times during the day. Identify your negative recitations and change them.

53

Pray During Night

Sura 17 Aya 79

And, additionally, rise from sleep and pray during the night and your Lord may well raise you to a glorious position.

Everyone has plans and dreams. You want to live a full and joyful life, and you want to help others. You want to be remembered as someone who made a difference. But you find that there are many barriers. You lack the resources you need to move forward. Also, you have habits that make you weak. Your willpower is not strong, and many fears haunt you. You are with people who do not share your vision and do not cooperate with you.

The dreamer inside us is the Divine Spirit. It inspires us with visions of perfection and tells us there are great possibilities. But the Spirit lives in an animal body which carries in it the memories of struggles of long years of evolution. Fear, laziness, and selfishness are embedded in our subconscious minds. Also, the subconscious has absorbed all the thoughts and impulses you were exposed to since your infancy, and much of this programming is negative.

The barrier to achieving your dreams is that the changes you want to make are overruled by the preexisting patterns in the subconscious. We all have had experiences to verify this for us. A common and simple example is like this: Suppose you have realized you are eating too many sweet foods and this is not good for you and you want to change this habit. You make a plan and a list of healthy foods you will substitute for the candies you are addicted to. Most people find it impossible to stick to such a plan because the habit of eating sweets is part of a pattern of pleasure rooted in the subconscious mind. The will has very little power over the subconscious.

The conscious mind is awake only when we are awake. The subconscious mind, however, works day and night. When we go to sleep, the conscious mind goes into hiding and the subconscious takes over.

The subconscious mind, because of its deep roots in existence, is the channel through which communication between man and God occurs. What you can place in your subconscious is immediately transmitted to God.

When you are close to sleep, you are slipping from a conscious state into the subconscious. Prayer at this time is highly effective because it has the possibility of reaching deep into your subconscious. Similarly, there is opportunity when you awaken, because you are coming out of your subconscious and the window to it is still partially open, so what you say at this time can penetrate into the subconscious and be submitted to God directly.

One method of reaching the subconscious is through repetition. If you focus on the same wish again and again through repetitive prayer for a long time, it will gain enough thrust and enter your subconscious.

This aya teaches another method for reprogramming your subconscious. Discipline yourself to awaken during the night from sleep and pray. You are very close to God in this state, and what you will say at this time has a very high possibility of being manifested. If you practice this method, your life can become an example of shining glory.

The night prayer was a key aspect of Prophet Muhammad's practice, and he spoke of its power frequently, as illustrated by the following four examples:

God, your Lord descends to the earth in the last third of the night and says, Who is asking something of Me so I can grant it to him, and who is seeking forgiveness of Me that I can forgive him?

A person is closest to God during the last third portion of the night. If at all possible for you to awaken and remember God at this time, then make sure you do so.

The prayer of Prophet David was the best in the eyes of God. He used to sleep only the first half of the night, pray for the next third of the night, and rest again during its last portion.

The night is long. Do not make it short with sleep.

Prayer is the greatest resource that a person of wisdom possesses. There are simple rules to follow to make your prayer effective. First, your prayer should be authentic for you. That is, it must emanate from your heart; it must reflect your own deeply held desires and goals. Second, it must be stated in the positive. That is, you ask for good for yourself and others. And third, you must have faith that God will grant your prayer. Prophet Muhammad said, *God always responds to your supplication. He will grant you what you ask for, or if He deems what you ask to be harmful for you, He will grant you something better than what you asked for.*

People who do not understand prayer often make it a ritual speaking of words they do not understand or relate to. This only conveys meaninglessness to their subconscious and manifests as confusion in their lives.

For your prayer to be authentic, you have to compose it yourself. You can learn from the examples of role models, but render it in your own words. It has to relate to your life. Think of all aspects of your life: your spirituality, your family, your health, your finances, your career, your character traits, the type of person you want to become, the contribution you want to make to the world. Write these desires in positive and clear language and memorize it. This is your prayer.

People who are confused about prayer and who have not experienced its benefits usually consider it a resource of last resort. When their life is stuck and everything they could think of and tried did not work, they say, "What else can we do in this situation except pray?"

People who understand the wisdom of prayer know its power and use it proactively and continuously to dissolve barriers and to shape their lives.

Waking up in the middle of the night is not easy in the beginning. It requires control over your sleep. Prophet Muhammad prayed that God give him the capacity to wake up in the night. His prayer was answered, and he used to pray at night. You can follow the same path and make the aspiration to pray at night part of your current prayer.

It is bound to happen sooner or later that one night

you will wake up during the middle of the night. You will not plan it, but something will happen that will awaken you. Such an experience is a gift from God. Be grateful that you have this opportunity. Wash your face, compose yourself, and use this time to talk to God about what you desire. This can open doors for you that you never previously could have imagined.

54

Pray Like This

Sura 17 Ayas 80–81

And say: "O my Lord! Cause me to enter in a true and sincere manner, and cause me to leave in a true and sincere manner, and grant me, out of Your grace, sustaining strength!"

And say: "The Truth has now come, and falsehood has withered away: for, behold, all falsehood is bound to wither!"

First, we note that these two verses illustrate two different styles of prayer. Aya 80 is a supplication, or a request, while Aya 81 is an assertion, or an affirmation. Many people are familiar with supplication as a form of prayer, but as Aya 81 shows here, making a statement is also prayer.

The power of prayer is in the power of human speech uttered with conviction and internalized by repetition. The human spirit is always in communication with God. In both types of prayer, we express faith in this communion. In one case, you request with the conviction that God hears you and will grant your request. In the second case, you express faith that your assertion resonates with the Divine Spirit.

These ayas teach us to seek two valuable insights. Let us consider them one by one.

And say: "O my Lord! Cause me to enter in a true and sincere manner, and cause me to leave in a true and sincere manner, and grant me, out of Your grace, sustaining strength!"

Everything we undertake has a lofty purpose associated with it. This is true of prayer, relationship with a person, a business, a project, a course of study, or volunteer work. The outcome for us depends on the motivation or intention we bring to what we are doing. Manipulation and duplicity often brings quick success but long-term unhappiness. Working with sincerity of purpose brings long-term fulfillment. The most basic spiritual quality is sincerity, and this supplication is to attain sincerity in everything we do.

Our intentions have layers. I can convince myself that I am sincere, but without having done my spiritual homework, this would be only at the surface level. Other impulses that are ingrained in my person, such as selfishness, greed, and pride, my neuroses and fears, they also become attached to my motivation and come into play as I interact with others.

Lack of awareness of our intentions is a major cause of life-failure for a large number of people.

Consider, for example, two people who are getting married. It is reasonable to say that in most cases the two are sincere in their superficial intentions of commitment to building a happy life together. However, as they live together, the deeper and previously hidden traits of selfishness and insincerity that are mixed up with their motivations come into play. Unless each does the work to discipline the inferior impulses, the relationship will become dysfunctional or fall apart.

The same dynamics can be experienced in organizations of more than two people, whether in a mosque, a business, or a government.

"Submission to God," a phrase often used to translate the Arabic word *Islam*, is the conscious expression of one's sincere intention to serve God, as opposed to serving one's ego. One important vehicle for achieving the state of submission is through regular prayer. In Al-Fateha, the canonical prayer, we make the following assertion addressing God:

"It is You alone we serve, and it is Your help we seek."

It is a declaration of the intention of rising above selfishness, to orient one's self to the larger purpose of serving God. We serve God by serving His creatures and by making the world a better place. If a phrase like this is uttered consciously and repeatedly, it is eventually internalized, and one's intention is "surrendered to God," and the person thus becomes a "Muslim."

Please read the aya again and note that the supplication to be made more sincere is accompanied by a request for strength.

In a culture of dishonesty and manipulation the focus is on short-term gains. A person of sincere and ethical motives is often regarded with suspicion in such an environment. Pressures and temptations are brought to him to become like others. If you do not get the message, many people become hostile to you and take steps to harm you. It takes extraordinary moral strength to live a life of sincere purpose. This strength can come to you from God if you are committed to serving Him.

In every enterprise, in every career, in every relationship, and in every aspect of life, there is a point of entry and there is a time of exit. It is a great merit to have sincere motivations when we begin an enterprise. It is a much greater achievement that your purpose and your motivation remain positive and sincere when you leave it. This is possible only if you develop the ability to be detached from your efforts. If you do things for personal or ego-centered motivations, the criticisms and hostility you will get from others will affect you adversely. Only to the extent that you are anchored in the belief that you are doing your job as a servant of God will you be insulated from the negative reactions of others. This will enable you to maintain your goodwill and sincerity of purpose when you exit the effort you were engaged in.

Let us now consider the insight in Aya 81.

And say: "The Truth has now come, and falsehood has withered away: for, behold, all falsehood is bound to wither!"

Everyone's consciousness is a mixture of truth and falsehood. To the extent we are anchored in the truth, we express love, faith, generosity, optimism, and service. The part of us that is stuck with falsehood makes us act with arrogance, greed, selfishness, and cruelty.

Every time we speak the affirmation in this aya, the truth in us is strengthened a little bit and the falsehood becomes a little weaker. If we repeat it, again and again, then gradually, we become embedded in good and our false assumptions lose their grip.

It is important to say this affirmation for the world also. Let there be more truth in the world and less falsehood. Let there be more knowledge and less superstition. Let there be more love, generosity, and faith in the hearts of people everywhere and let the false values of disdain, prejudice, and animosity wither away everywhere.

55

God Has Many Names

Sura 17 Aya 110

Say: "Invoke Allah, or invoke the Rahman: by whichever name you invoke Him, all His names are beautiful."

It is a historical fact that belief in the one invisible God was discovered by people in many parts of the world. But in every culture, people became possessive about the name of God they used and considered the names used by others as false. A large part of human history is about conflicts between people who used different names for God and different forms of worship.

The Arabs at the time of Prophet Muhammad were familiar with "Allah" as the name of God, and so it is used extensively in the Quran. The Jews in Arabia used the name Rahman (The Merciful) for God, and Prophet Muhammad adopted this name also in his teachings. The Arabs were bewildered by this and criticized the Prophet for using an alien name for God. This aya points out that God has many names that you can call Him. There is no need to insist that only one is correct and others are wrong.

Most of the alienation between cultures is not about essential values but about chauvinistic feelings related to symbols such as the name of God, forms of worship, buildings, flags, language, etc. People every where believe in God, prayer, generosity, and love, but they express their beliefs using different symbols. The hostility and wars have been about the empty pride associated with symbols.

One example of historical hostility because of religious symbolism is between Hindus and Muslims in South Asia. Many wise people pointed out that the basic beliefs of the two religions are similar, but this has been ignored by religious and political zealots for centuries, resulting in prolonged strife. In terms of their views of God, both traditions espouse the worship of one Supreme Being with many attributes. The different gods and goddesses of Hinduism represent various functions of one supreme Divinity. And the Quran also called God by many names, each representing a different trait. Many of the attributes by which the Hindu gods are known have their exact equivalents in the Quran. Examples are given in the table below.

Hindu Divine Name	**Attribute Expressed in English**	**Muslim Divine Name**
Brahma	The Creator	Al-Khaliq
Vishnu	The Sustainer	Al-Razzaq
Shiva	The Destroyer	Ad-Darr
Saraswati	The Wise	Al-Hakeem
Lakshmi	Giver of Abundance	Al-Mughni
Durga	The Powerful	Al-Muhaymin
Rama	The Ideal King	Al-Malik
Krishna	The Lover	Al-Wadud
Ganesh	Remover of Obstacles	Al-Fattah
Hanuman	The Strong	Al-Qawi

The important question about God is not that you are proud of the way He is represented in your culture, but how effective your belief is in helping you become a better person. Has your faith guided you to become a source of compassion for all people? If not, there is more to learn about faith. Each religious tradition began with one person who learned to relate to God in a way that transformed his life and created major positive impact on others. The purpose of religious teaching is to make us aware that such an experience is possible for each of us, and how to achieve it.

56

Live to Create Beauty

Sura 18 Ayas 7–8

Surely what is on the earth We made to enhance its beauty, so that We can test to see whose actions are the finest.

And surely We shall turn what is on it into dry dust.

Keeping the Arabic words related to beauty, the first aya is: "Surely what is on the earth We made for its *zeenat* so that we can test to see whose actions are *ahsan*." *Zeenat* means adornment and decoration. *Ahsan* means something that is pleasing, refined, elegant, and attractive. The two words convey similar notions. Everything that God has made is beautiful, because beauty is a divine trait. In Aya 7, He asks us to appreciate, preserve, and enhance this beauty. This is a test of how we live. Our actions either add to the splendor that is creation or they diminish it. One of the names of God is *Al-Musawwir*, the Artist. Like all His other traits, the Artist is present in all human beings. All of us have within us the ability to create beauty, to express what we see with new perspectives.

When we talk of beauty in nature, we often think of special scenes that appeal to us, such as the splendor of colors at sunset, the vista of the vast ocean from a beach, beautiful flowers in a garden, or a flock of birds flying in a symmetrical pattern. This aya says, however, that beauty and magnificence are in everything that has been created. It is not confined to a few spots. We need to expand our awareness.

Beauty in creation is a test of how people direct their awareness. If you notice and appreciate it, you will see more and more of it everywhere. It will be natural for you to praise God. But if you are self-centered, you can be focused on your ailments and obsessions and be oblivious to the grandeur that surrounds you in every direction.

Have you noticed that people who live in a city go for vacations in the mountains? They are enthralled by the splendor in the countryside and by the sight of the sun rising over the mountain every morning. They feel exhilarated by the freshness of the air and the clearness of the sky. However, people who live near the mountains do not notice the beauty in their surroundings. They perceive splendor when they visit the city. They notice the well dressed people, the magnificent buildings, the glamour of wealth displayed in the city. The city folk, however, have become accustomed to these things and are oblivious to them.

Artists create works of beauty by taking an item from nature and displaying it on canvas, bringing out the details they noticed in it. Artists are teachers for mankind because they bring to our attention what we fail to see ourselves.

There is great beauty in how God has made you. Your

height, the pigment of your skin, the size of your limbs, and the proportion of your features are the handiwork of God. Appreciating this fact, and being grateful for who you are makes a huge difference in one's life. It is the basis of healthy self-esteem. People who think well of themselves are happy and self-confident.

Those who think of themselves as flawed in how they are—too tall or too short, too dark or too pale—become neurotic. In every culture, there is a certain body type, a certain look that is popular. Many people compare themselves with the model they see in TV commercials and feel inferior. In this way, they afflict themselves. They damage their self-esteem and become unhappy. This is a form of ingratitude. It is like saying to God: "You messed up in making me. I wish You were smarter when You had the idea about me."

The only cure for poor self-esteem is to negate the ideas that generate these feelings in us. You have to believe this aya when it says that God has made everything on the earth in order to beautify it. You are one of His creations, and, therefore, you are an adornment for the world. You have to reject all thoughts that oppose this fact.

Each of us is part of the magnificence God has created on the earth, and He asks us to increase it. Life is a test to see who lives in the best way. So an important measure of spiritual merit of any action is its aesthetic quality. The way you look, the clothes you wear, how you smell, the way you talk, the way you do your work, your home, your backyard—all of these should add to the beauty of the world.

It is important to look good so that it is a pleasure for others to meet you. The feelings others have about you are influenced by your appearance. An unkempt appearance turns people off. It is narrated in the books of Hadith that Prophet Muhammad took great care for his appearance. He carried a comb and a small mirror in his pocket so that he could groom himself whenever needed. He was fond of perfume, used it himself, and recommended it to his companions.

I have known people who take great care to look good when they go out of the house but stay disheveled in the home, not realizing how it affects their intimate relationships. Your appearance creates an atmosphere about you. The people who live with you see you the most, and they are affected the most by how you keep yourself. Many people complain that his or her mate does not take an interest in them, while not paying attention to their own appearance in the home.

Of course, enhancing your personal beauty is not confined to just the physical appearance but also to your conversation and the way you act toward people. In Sura 17, Aya 53 it is said: *"Speak only what is best."* Learning to choose the best words and to speak them in an attractive tone of voice are important tools each of us has been given to make the world a more pleasant place.

The way we do our work has an aesthetic quality. Whether you are operating a machine, or designing a project, or working on a farm, or cooking for the family, it can be done in a sloppy way or in a way marked by elegance. Taking pride in our work, bringing it to a good conclusion, doing it cheerfully—they are aspects of doing our work well.

The way your living space looks, whether it is one room or a big house, is an indicator of how much you value your role in making the world more beautiful. Keeping your space clean is the essential first step in beautifying your environment.

Beauty is the opposite of entropy. If you don't make an effort, you have disorder and sloppiness. Creation of beauty is a spiritual value because it requires proactivity. Laziness results in sloppiness, but creation of beauty and elegance requires work. You have to overcome resistance. There is resistance within all of us in the form of laziness. Prophet Muhammad said that laziness is from Satan. Whenever we overcome laziness within us, we defeat Satan. That is how life is a test. On any given day, I am either going to be lazy or make an effort to make the world a better place.

Beauty in the world is also a test because you can be consumed by it if you are passive. If you are not seeking to create it but only drink it, it can overwhelm your life. I have known people who enjoyed listening to music so much they had little energy left to do anything positive with their time. You can be so mesmerized by sights of beautiful women that you cannot concentrate on your work. You can be so addicted to food and drink that it will ruin your health.

In Aya 8, we are told: *"And surely We shall turn what is on it into dry dust."* We are reminded that the beautiful things that exist around us will eventually disappear, so we should value and appreciate them while they are here. Life is brief. Each day is a gift, so live it well before it is gone forever.

One reason we are not able to see or appreciate the beauty in creation is because we tend to be in haste. We are always rushing from place to place. We look at many things superficially but rarely stop to experience them deeply. Have you seen a man rapidly gulping down his lunch of half-chewed food? He is anxious to have as much as he can in a short time. He has little opportunity to appreciate the delicate flavors in what he is eating. Lunch would be a much more enjoyable experience if he ate less, took smaller bites, and chewed the food thoroughly. His senses of smell, touch, and taste would then more fully participate in the act of eating.

Learn to pace yourself, live fully in the moment, experience the beauty in creation, and enhance it is the message of these ayas.

57

Trapped by Your Thinking

There are numerous ayas in the Quran saying that God has sealed people's hearts or made them blind so they cannot see the truth. Here we consider one such aya to explore the wisdom in such statements:

Sura 18 Aya 57

And who could be more in darkness than he who is told of the ayas from his Lord and he turns away from them, unmindful of what his hands have sent before. Surely We have placed veils over their hearts, lest they understand, and a deafness in their ears; and if you call them to guidance they will never allow themselves to be guided.

A superficial reading of this aya would suggest that God punishes people by abandoning them and making them impervious to guidance. In reality, it is an expression of the law of attraction. If you engage in thoughts that lack faith, more thoughts of the same type come to you, and then still more thoughts, and eventually, your views become entrenched in a lack of faith. You can no longer see alternatives to what you are thinking. The Arabic metaphor "*what his hands have sent before*" means what he did earlier bears fruit later. Thus, previous choices have solidified certain ideas in his mind, and when a better way is offered he finds it unappealing and rejects it.

Perhaps you had an experience like this. You learned something new that helped you. You tell a friend about it because you want to help him. You are sure it can change his life for the better, as it did for you. But he rejects it outright. He behaves as if he cannot hear the simple truth that is so obviously clear to you. This is because a different idea is deeply ingrained in his mind, and it clashes with what you are saying.

We are always thinking. But each thought is like a magnet. It attracts other thoughts like it. And when two thoughts of the same type are collected together in your mind, they act like a bigger magnet. They attract even more thoughts of the same type, and people who have similar thoughts. Unless we deliberately interrupt this process, it continues to expand in the mind like a snowball, and in the course of time, the mind becomes engulfed in this type of thought, which crystallizes into a belief. This process has been called the law of attraction by modern spiritual teachers.

But where do these other thoughts we attract come from? Consider the thoughts that usually circulate in your mind. While some have arisen from what you have seen or heard, others are from the patterns stored in your nervous system you inherited from your parents. They, in turn, inherited many patterns of thinking and behavior from their parents. This chain of connections goes back into the infinite past. Your mental structure is linked to what was learned N generations ago, where N is greater than a million or ten million or any number. It continues to before there were human beings on the earth. There is an unbroken chain that connects every living person to the first life form. In this way, each of us has information stored within us which is the collective inheritance of all life. Carl Jung called it the collective consciousness. It is the vast reservoir of thoughts, ideas, impulses, and images that life has gathered through its development over eons. What we think in our conscious minds is only a very small portion of the thoughts in us. Most of these are in the subconscious mind where the collective consciousness resides.

Many people not only do not wish to listen to advice but are offended when offered advice. Not only they have a fixed way of thinking, they are also possessive about it. Their egos are tied up with how they are. When you tell them something good they say to themselves: "Who is this person to tell me what I should be doing?" They want to stay with 'their' ways and do not want any part of 'your' ways. Such people remain stuck in their ways, unless forced by extraordinary events to re-evaluate their assumptions.

It is a truly fortunate person who is open to counsel, and is open minded about new information. He or she weighs the facts, and decides on a recommendation based on merit, without prejudice about where the idea came from. Such a person grows by learning new ways, and gains resources to make life better for himself and others.

The way to live with faith is to always search for better ways. You want to break the old mold and believe that a better way is possible. You do not want to stay trapped in the condition described in this aya. You then become a student of wisdom, and your quest brings you better information and better ways of living. This search for continuous improvement is in the saying of Prophet Muhammad: *"If a day passes in which I do not learn something new, it is a day wasted from my life."* The belief that you can change yourself for the better is an expression of faith.

This aya is speaking of the tremendous resistance to change built up inside us because of the deep-rooted nature of our present views. That is why so many people who make new year resolutions are unable to follow through with them. In spite of well laid plans and good intentions, they keep going back to what they are used to. A practical lesson from this discussion is that if we wish to adopt a new habit, we have to work at it diligently. We have to be aware of the deep resistance we will encounter within ourselves. You have to think about your new idea again and again, so it sticks with you. Some of the proven ways of achieving this are:

1. You can pray that God gives you the strength to change your habit. Say, "God, please help me become a person who uses his time well." Or, "God, let me be someone who acquires useful knowledge every day." Repeat this prayer several times a day, until you find yourself acting accordingly.
2. You can make affirmations supporting your new thoughts and repeat them to yourself. For example, say, "I choose to eat what is healthy," or "I am the type of person who speaks well of others." Speak your affirmations several times a day. You can write your new resolutions on pieces of paper and carry them in your wallet, so that you see them several times in a day. Keep up this practice until you see the new habit

established in your behavior.

3. Write about the change you want to make in your journal. Write about the many benefits that will come to you if you succeed in establishing the new habit; how your self-image will improve, and how you will be a good role model for the people you know. Also, write about the loss that is bound to occur if you do not change. Do such writing every day until you see the change you have desired become established in you.
4. Prophet Muhammad taught his companions to see what they asked for in their imagination. It is a powerful method to make pictures in your mind in which you see yourself acting in the new way. Set aside ten minutes before you go to bed, or after you wake up, or after your lunch break to sit in a quiet place. Take a few deep breaths to let your mind settle. Then see yourself in your mind's eye doing as you have desired. Keep up with this practice until your new habit becomes a reality.

If you experiment with these four methods, you will find one of them easier to use than others. Adopt that method and work with it until you succeed. Your new way of thinking needs to be repeated until it attracts enough thoughts similar to it, so it can take root in you.

It is not usually possible to change your thinking, or behavior, without changing the company you keep. Consider a person who comes to the realization that he wants to stop speaking ill of others behind their back. This habit has probably been there in him for years and was formed in the family where he grew up. He is used to finding pleasure in judging people, and his friends and relatives do the same. Their conversation and their jokes are mostly at the expense of others. They will feel uncomfortable if he tries to change himself. Their conversation will no longer be smooth, and it is unlikely that he can change his habit if he keeps meeting the same people.

The law of attraction is a law that governs the human psyche. But notice that the aya says, "*We have placed veils over their hearts* ..." This is because God has made the laws which govern the world. Similarly, we know that clouds and rain are formed according to laws of physics. Since God has made the physical laws also, in the Quran God says, "We raise the winds that bring the clouds that produce rain." Thus, God speaks in the Quran as the cause of all that happens, each event taking place according to the laws He has made.

58

Ask Questions and Receive Answers

Sura 25 Aya 33
And no puzzling question do they bring to you but We will bring the truth in answer and the best explanation.

The nature of life is such that each of us faces situations where we are not sure how to proceed. There are conflicting options, and good evidence to support each of them. It is wise not to make a decision quickly in such a situation. Wait for a few days, or a few weeks, until an answer comes to you. This will be the best solution for the problem.

Prophet Muhammad used this method always. Whenever someone asked him a question he did not know the answer to, the Prophet would not respond immediately. The answer appeared to him in due course. Each of us can follow this habit of the Prophet and access God's wisdom to move our lives in the best possible direction.

Everyone knows we have sources of information outside of us. We can read and learn, and we can consult with experts who are knowledgeable about what we are looking for. But sometimes we don't get clear guidance from these outside sources of knowledge. In such a case, we can look for the source of wisdom within us.

There are two memory banks inside each of us. One is at the surface, the conscious mind where our current ideas and thoughts reside. The other is the subconscious mind where all there is to know is present. Everything that a person has ever thought or heard or done is recorded in the subconscious mind. Moreover, the subconscious mind also contains information inherited from previous generations. A useful way to think about the subconscious is this: You have inherited patterns of thinking from your parents. Your parents had inherited information from their parents, and they from their parents. This chain goes back to all the generations that have ever existed, to the first form of life. Thus, in each human being's mind, there is a storehouse of information collected from the experiences of countless ages of existence. Our intuition resides here. Each of us is connected to God through the subconscious mind.

Some people are startled by this discussion. They say:" If I ask questions and receive answers through inspiration, does it mean I have the same rank as Prophet Muhammad?" He was a prophet with a special relationship with God, and God revealed answers to him. It is not correct to say I can receive revelations like the Prophet. The answer to this question is that the subconscious is very deep, and Prophet Muhammad had the spiritual power to receive answers from a very deep level. Most people explore shallower depths. Their minds are clouded with noise. The source is the same for everyone, but different people access it to different levels of depth.

If you have a dominant purpose in life, your mind looks

for and collects information related to fulfilling your purpose. If there is no purpose, your mind absorbs all kinds of random information and images from the surroundings. This accumulated clutter is a barrier between the conscious and subconscious minds. When someone's mind is filled up with a thick layer of junk information, he or she is not able to perceive the messages coming from deeper awareness. Thus, it is said in Aya 14 of Sura 83: *"Their hearts are covered with rust because of what they do."*

Clutter is dissipated in solitude. If you develop the habit of spending time alone every day, your mind gradually becomes clear and you become aware of your deeper thoughts. Eventually, you can then see the channel through which your prayer is communicated to God.

Inspiration is like water bubbling from the floor of a spring. The water is coming up from an aquifer down below which has a huge amount of pure water. If the surface of the spring is clean, you can see the water bubbling up at the bottom. In places where the surface is opaque with dirt, we cannot see the depth. Similarly, we are always connected to inspiration, but we do not perceive it because our minds are filled with all kinds of haphazard thoughts. Those who learn to quiet their minds can feel the inspiration guiding them all the time.

There is another technique for getting guidance from your deep self. If you want to know the answer to a problem, write the questions you have in your journal. Also write possible answers that you know of as much as possible. The answers you know may not be satisfactory and may conflict with each other, but it does not matter. Write them down nonetheless. At this stage, you are just entering your data into the computer. Then leave this problem alone. Don't think or talk about it for a couple of weeks. Eventually, go back to your journal and read what you wrote. Then start writing about possible answers and soon, the correct answer will come to you. If the answer you receive is not satisfactory, then come back to it again after another week and you will have a more mature answer.

Artists, writers, scientists, and other creative people know the truth taught in this aya. They know that if you ask questions about a problem, then answers come to you through inspiration later. Actually, somebody becomes a successful artist or a writer or a scientist only after he or she has learned to tap their subconscious for inspiration.

Experience shows that answers come in a number of ways. They can come as words or images in our consciousness, or in a dream sequence, or it comes from the outside with someone giving the answer you are looking for. Sometimes the answers to our questions appear quickly and sometimes with a delay. Since God chooses the timing, we trust that it is perfect for the situation.

59

Religious Tolerance

Sura 22 Aya 67

To every community We have given ways of worship which they observe. Therefore, do not let them draw you into disputes on this matter, but invite people to your Lord, for you are on the right way.

An attitude of religious tolerance is described in this verse. It is in recognizing the authenticity of the different ways of worship found among different people. Different religious traditions represent different possible paths to God-consciousness, and it is a mistake to argue with people about their traditions and rituals.

The opposite attitude is to consider our own particular ritual of prayer as the only one acceptable to God. An extension of this belief is that all other ways are misguided and those who follow them are bound for hell. This belief is the root of intolerance. It has caused enmity and bloodshed between religious communities for centuries.

When Muslims were a new community on Long Island

in the 1980s, they formed an association but did not have a building of their own. They approached a church, and the elders of the church gladly gave them permission to hold their prayers in the church. The church elders demonstrated the wisdom conveyed by this aya.

In a few years, the Muslim community collected enough funds to build a mosque of their own and moved their congregation to the new building. A few years later, a group of Ismaili Muslims approached them because they were new to the area and did not yet have a building of their own. They asked the officials of the mosque for permission to hold their prayer services in the mosque. The mosque officials denied them permission. "The Ismailies are misguided people, and their prayer is not correct," said one of the mosque trustees. The mosque trustees did not understand the message of this aya.

This attitude is common in mosques throughout the world. It is at the root of the deep suspicion many Muslims display toward peoples of other faiths, not only non-Muslims, but also Muslims with alternate traditions. Minority Muslim populations such as the Ismailies, the Druze, the Baha'is, and the Ahmadies feel isolated and persecuted in many Muslim countries. An essential part of Muslim reformation is to recognize that tolerance is not a Western idea, but it is a universal concept from the Quran. It is beneficial to everyone who practices it. Societies where people accept each other irrespective of religious beliefs are strong and dynamic, and societies where there is intolerance among faith groups are splintered and weak.

The attitude of self-righteous intolerance comes partly from feelings of insecurity about your own ways. If you have not thought about your rituals of worship deeply and are not sure why you do them, you feel threatened by the alternatives offered by others. If, on the other hand, you are sure that *you are on the right way* as the aya above points out, you will gladly acknowledge that other people have their own authentic ways of worshipping God.

CPSIA information can be obtained at www.ICGtesting.com
Printed in the USA
LVOW12*1305190913

353166LV00005B/277/P